Defenses

Overcoming Defensive Barriers
In Restoring Personal Worth

Russ Llewellyn, Th.M., Ph.D.

ISBN 978-0-9841249-8-5

FIRST PRINTING

Russ Llewellyn, Th.M., Ph.D.
Address: PO Box 22
San Carlos, CA, USA, 94070
Phone: 650-595-4500

E-mail: DrRussLlewellyn@wholepersonpublications.com

Cover Design by www.itlayer.com
Book design and typesetting by Chris Holm

Whole Person
PUBLICATIONS

Defenses

Overcoming Defensive Barriers
In Restoring Personal Worth

Russ Llewellyn, Th.M., Ph.D.

Contents

The Message of this Book.. 1

1 Healing Rejection's Armor: The False Self.................... 3

2 Restoring Worth 22

3 When Love Hurts.. 42

4 Hidden Personal Needs... 56

I Pray That You Gain Life's Prize 71

APPENDICES

God Requests Your Personal RSVP 77

Your Relationship With God... 79

The Message of this Book

Overcoming Defensive Barriers
In Restoring Personal Worth

DEFENSES CREATE RESISTANCE TO OUR FULLY KNOWING OR ACCEPT-
ING OURSELVES. Rejection, emotional pain, betrayal, abuse, and
lack of nurture or affection become internalized and defended against.
Defenses can be part of a false self we create in order to live with what is
not acceptable to us about ourselves. How are we going to overcome such
defensiveness to heal?

If we were given positive loving experiences in which people trust us,
we naturally develop emotional openness. Intimacy and security in relationships is easy for such people.

Sin has affected our ability to know ourselves. If we really want to
know ourselves thoroughly, it takes humility and God's presence in our
lives. We need help in overcoming what is unacceptable to us about ourselves.

Being needy and not knowing it is like being lost. Needs can make us
vulnerable. Defensiveness is often directed against the helplessness and
weakness of our needs. Sometimes those defenses are administered with
brutal force. We hurt from the continued self-rejection.

Accepting that God cherishes us while He provides for us moves us
toward being able to cherish ourselves and accept our needs. That's a step
toward self-esteem.

Love can sometimes be a real pain. When we've been hurt or our
trust betrayed by previous blows, love can trigger intense emotional pain.
There's a difference between self-boundaries and defenses. In fact, it takes

a conscious decision to experience previous emotional pain to heal and overcome defensiveness.

Defensiveness contains issues of eternal glory and self worth. Things that remain hidden and unexposed (unconscious) detract from our eternal worth. Things that are revealed and become light (consciousness) become transformed and a part of our glorious inheritance. You will read several personal stories, including mine, in which things that were hidden in unconscious motivation are healed.

It's worth the often difficult challenge to work through defensiveness issues! Intimacy with God, ourselves and others is possible when we love enough to overcome our defenses.

Chapter 1

Healing Rejection's Armor:
The False Self

༈

"O Lord, you have searched me and you know me ....
you perceive my thoughts from afar .... you are
familiar with all my ways. Before a word is on my
tongue you know it completely, O Lord ... such
knowledge is too wonderful for me, too lofty for me
to attain." Psalm 139:1-6

ARE YOU OPEN TO FINDING YOUR FALSE SELF?

Do you cherish a self-image that makes you acceptable? Do you tend to think you're worthless, bad, wrong or a mistake? Either motivation creates a false self. God's presence will help you move beyond self-rejection to love and accept your true self.

We need humility to know and fashion an accurate estimate of ourselves. And we need God. When we're open to living in God's presence, we can learn to know ourselves fully. To some, that may not seem like a big plus. But it's the first step we need to take in recovering God's design for wholeness in our lives.

We need to ask God's help in knowing ourselves because He loves and knows and cares about us infinitely more than we know and care about ourselves. The truth is, there are some things we don't want to know about ourselves. So we need His help! Of course it takes humility to ask from God what we can't give ourselves.

What picture do we like to hold of ourselves? You could feel toward yourself like someone contentedly gazing at a mountain meadow filled with wildflowers. Or you could see yourself as a mud-caked person stuck in a slimy pit. Any self-image, whether positive or negative, may be built on a false view of ourselves. *The false self is any view of ourselves we hold for self-protective reasons.*

In order to overcome the false self, we must admit a healthy dose of God's loving presence into our lives. Sometimes this grace will be mediated through a loving and accepting person. Without such grace, knowing the unpleasant truth about ourselves might lead us to internal harshness of self-rejection. *Overcoming the false self demands humility* in our seeing the self-fiction we hold, which either we or others have created. Humility can acknowledge the truth of our failure to live up to a grand self-ideal and will remove our grip from a nasty self-notion.

Anxiety motivates our hiding our true selves behind a defensive door so others wouldn't guess what we're hiding. We could construct a lofty, acceptable, better-than-us self. Our defenses could also fabricate a no-good self. (Actually, most people with this awful view of themselves believe that it has been "dished up" to them by someone else, who has then demanded that they own it and eat it.) Humility opens the door in a relaxed way that our defenses have anxiously or angrily closed.

Humility reopens us to relationships and trust – most importantly, trust in God. With the loving truth from God about ourselves, we can construct a durable self-esteem.

It's like our home entry way. The front porch entry to our home shows how defenses work. Beautiful wide brick steps lead to our front door. One section of bricks started to crack and pull apart as earth settled unevenly. Cosmetic patchwork didn't fix the problem because they pulled apart again. To create a permanent solution, we dismantled the steps, put in a durable foundation, and rebuilt them so they would last. It doesn't matter why we built them flawed in the first place. We had to come to grips with what was and do something to fix it.

In my case, I grew up with perfectionism and not only absorbed its values, but passed it on to our children. One reacted by absorbing it, one by rebelling against it. He spent a lot of time in "time-out" growing up.

I believe we have two options in building defenses to protect our self ideal.

We can either: 1) hide what we hate; or 2) hide what we treasure. If we hide what we hate about ourselves, we're likely to show something sweet and likable on the surface that declares, "You don't need to look any deeper, I'm a nice person." If we hide what we treasure, we're likely to show something nasty to the world that says, "Stay away!"

This may be surprising to you, but some people actually prefer and like to hold a negative self-image. They emblazon negativity on their tee-shirts or tattoo their bodies with it. That's their honest-to goodness choice! The motivation? They disarm other's negativity about them by beating others to the punch. Where does this self-blasting come from? They dislike themselves because they've swallowed negative beliefs about themselves that seem more "true," and now it's become a conviction.

T.M. (she goes by her initials), whom you've met before, as a little girl was conditioned with cruelty and told she didn't deserve the air she breathed because of two inexcusable offenses: she's a girl, and she's ugly. The first is true, the second isn't. Try telling her that! As an adult, she cringes when I direct positive feelings or thoughts her way. It actually feels quite painful for her to hear my kind words; she describes them as "shooting darts at her." She doesn't want to believe or receive them. She calls positive statements about her "lies." The mirror I try to hold up to her is that she absorbed negativity about herself – anger and rejection directed at her – as though it were the truth about herself.

Anchoring herself to that false position protected T.M. from more hurt when she was being brutalized and humiliated. This false view serves to protect her from feeling the intensity of her trembling, emotional pain and the searing hot anger she feels toward her abuser. It's time now to heal and to leave the protection of the false bad self and realize that her true self has been lost. She'd hidden it. She has turbulent, painful emotions to digest and faulty, imprisoning beliefs to correct. God loves that crushed and shamed little girl and the adult who takes comfort hiding from people in her darkened, shades-down bedroom. She has no current external need to hide in the "bad-me" closet she's created. Truth be known, now she's hiding more from herself than others. Hiding only serves to protect her from unwanted emotions and stunting beliefs about herself. Once accepted, her healing path has weeks and months of tears ahead. The false self, while painful, seems like an easier place to hide.

Then, there's the other extreme. If T.M. is too bad to be true, Meg is too good to be true. Meg, whom I've worked with, said, "I like myself very well, thank you!" What she meant was, "Don't think I'm going to let you mess with my positive feelings about myself!" What she loved was killing her with performance pressure! Those ideals she was married to were like wedding vows to her soul. She had a choice to change what she prized or die trying to reach the unattainable. I was talking to Meg as though she were married to her attractive, false self. "First find it. Then divorce it! Instead, embrace a self with whom you could become friends. God made you in His image so you could become like Him."

We first learn from others what is unacceptable about us. Often we decide to dislike those very things in ourselves. This miserable concoction creates human defensiveness. Now, we need to hide from ourselves what was originally rejectable to others.

I'M UNACCEPTABLE, SO I NEED A FALSE SELF

The unconscious is the storage bin for the unacceptable self. The sad, anxious and sometimes angry truth is, we want to hide in this emotional and spiritual darkness. We want to pull the covers of darkness over our heads and be lost to ourselves. We shrink from fully knowing ourselves, "the truth, the whole truth and nothing but the truth, so help us God." We create a defensive false self that blocks us from knowing ourselves completely or freely walking in God's presence. In this dilemma, God is our surest hope. Here's how the psalmist, David, describes this motivation to hide. "If I say, 'Surely the darkness will hide me and the light become night around me,' even the darkness will not be dark to you; the night will shine like the day, for darkness is as light to you. For you created my inmost being; you knit me together in my mother's womb."[1]

Why would we want to recover such hidden knowledge about ourselves unless God first instilled that desire? We must first experience God's limitless forgiveness and embracing love or we have no foundation for forgiving, loving and accepting ourselves. *It takes humility to discover the unwanted truth about ourselves. The truth is that some part about ourselves is unacceptable to us.* We would reject ourselves if we knew the truth. That unwanted truth is hidden in our unconscious. It's like picking up a room and storing all the mess in the closet because company is coming. It takes humility, courage, love and acceptance to search for the messy truth about ourselves. God's Comforter, the Holy Spirit of Truth, leads us into all truth. *It is only truth that frees us.* We must learn to walk in His presence to live in freedom.

GOD'S LOVE CREATES EAGERNESS IN US TO KNOW OURSELVES

Life brings storms. We human beings need a safe harbor in which to dock when life tumbles us on it's waves. No matter where we've come from, God's love is that safe harbor. We can be protected in His love. Once we are convinced God fully knows and fully loves us, we must receive within us His powerful filling and transforming love. *Once we hold the conviction God thoroughly loves us, we will have the courage to fully know God. Only then will we be eager for Him to reveal the complete truth about ourselves to us so we can fully know ourselves too.* We need to walk in the warm sunlight of God's presence to leave the cold comfort of the false self behind.

David again speaks of the secure love of being in God's presence and being known. "O LORD, you have searched me and you know me. You know when I sit and when I rise; you perceive my thoughts from afar. You discern my going out and my lying down; you are familiar with all my ways. Before a word is on my tongue you know it completely, O LORD. You hem me in – behind and before; you have laid your hand upon me. Such knowledge is too wonderful for me, too lofty for me to attain. Where can I go from your Spirit? Where can I flee from your presence? If I go up to the heavens, you are there; if I make my bed in the depths, you are there. If I rise on the wings of the dawn, if I settle on the far side of the sea, even there your hand will guide me, your right hand will hold me fast."[2]

Without God in the picture, we self-protectively and naturally want to build our self-esteem on the false self. It takes great humility to build it rather on the truth that God loves us at our worst and cultivate our awareness of His welcoming presence. Then we will request that God stretch our minds and hearts as David did so we will know both God and ourselves, "Search me, O God, and know my heart; test me and know my anxious thoughts. See if there is any offensive way in me, and lead me in the way everlasting.[3]

"Love liberates us... by letting us see that the ideal self does not have to be the one thing we need to become. It convinces us that God accepts our actual self in forgiveness and adoption as his children. God's love then shows that our actual, blemished self is the only self that can be an agent of love."[4]

We must let God build within us a strength to love which is beyond our meager powers. Only then we can lovingly accept ourselves, once we find what's unacceptable within us. That supernatural ability to love comes from God alone. Sometimes that love of God is mediated, in that it comes from another human being who loves us as God does. Sometimes God communicates His love directly through revelation by His Spirit, through an angel or in dreams. However he sends the message, we must first receive the love God has for us so we can build our self-esteem on the love and valuing God has for us. If not, we will create an image of ourselves which will be acceptable to us and try to live up to or become that image. *Such a construction project makes the false self into an idol which we worship. To protect that false self, we will prize character traits of pride in our own strength[5] or gratification of our wants.[6]* We must surrender the false self and let God preside over it's dismantling to attain an esteem from the God Who loves us unconditionally.[7] He sees the beauty He put within us when He created us.

Our daughter Donna said, "I never knew how much I prided myself on my strength, my balance and agility." The effects of the cancerous brain tumor caused her to lose her balance, bloodying her knee on a hike with her family to Vernal Falls in Yosemite. Her energy spent, she reached the bottom of the falls and sent her husband Gary and her two daughters up the rest of the hike to the top of the falls. "I sat on the side of the trail. Tears flowed fully as I watched other climbers go up so easily, some chunky, some in sandals. My pride shattered. I should be able to do this hike! This should be a piece of cake! I've climbed up the backside of Half Dome! As I listened to the thunderous sounds of the waterfalls crashing on the rocks below, I felt like God was doing the same thing with my pride, crushing it."

I asked her what she's done with those lessons since then. "I kept wanting to take back the part I surrendered," she replied. "I still wanted to pride myself in my strength." Then she quoted an idea from *Broken In The Right Places* by Alan Nelson, "You have to let go of who you are in order that God can fill you with Him."

CREATION'S UNBROKEN FRIENDSHIP WITH GOD AND OURSELVES

I don't know if you've ever thought of it this way, but human consciousness has spiritual origins. In the first days after creation when Adam and Eve walked the earth, they shared joy, gladness, intimacy, and I'm sure, laughter with God their Father in an unbroken friendship. They were the crowning glory of His creation, the joy and delight of their Father's heart, the apple of His eye. He approved of the people He had made, taking great pleasure in His son and daughter, Adam and Eve. He pronounced them "very good" along with the rest of His creation.

All awareness they experienced was full, instantaneous and conscious. They knew only openness within themselves and between themselves and God. There was no need for defenses. They had no fear, guilt, shame. There was nothing unacceptable about them and they did not judge themselves negatively. There was no need for an unconscious. They lived and walked in the full light of consciousness. No knowledge or truth about them was hidden and out of sight. Truth was undivided and pure – undistorted. They were full of light, enlightened human beings. Adam and Eve initially experienced no darkness within the self.

SELF-DOUBT AND FEAR BIRTHED THE NEED FOR AN UNCONSCIOUS

Then came the temptation to doubt their belief in God and to doubt themselves. The temptation to know evil was an attack on a basic truth about the goodness of God and goodness in themselves. Regarding themselves, it was the temptation to doubt that they were good, and to fear that their goodness was insufficient. Satan's challenge to them was that they needed to know more than they did, namely "evil." This attack implied that their goodness wasn't adequate. The Tempter raised doubts about themselves. Could it be that they did not have some essential knowledge that was desirable? Was God good if He was holding out on them?

In doubting God's goodness, they lost confidence in their own goodness as well. In yielding to temptation, basic trust was broken in God's loving care and goodness. Our first parent's choices shattered our ability to fully know or trust God or to fully know or trust ourselves. We human beings became divided in our consciousness. We could not fully companion with God, and became competitors with Him. Nor could we fully befriend ourselves, because our nature housed a new adversary. We were at war with ourselves. We became our own worst enemy.

To live in this conflict, we would have to hide some of the evidence. There was a split in our consciousness. Part was light and known. Part was dark and hidden. We chose to hide what was unacceptable about ourselves in the darkness of the unconscious.

KNOWING BOTH GOOD AND EVIL IN THE SELF

You may wonder why I'm leading you through this spectacular spiritual wasteland of our human past. It's because we must know that we're in a desert before we will seek the oasis God put there and discover that our human thirsts are really our lost thirst for God. When we long for His path and wholeheartedly seek Him, we will surely find him.[8] Lost desert wanderings are only designed for those unwilling to submit to God's way out. So please bear with me a bit more in my talking about how evil affected the self, as well as God's way out.

What our first parents did still affects us today. The knowledge of evil meant that they aligned themselves with the power that was against the One True God and against the truth of the self. There was a whole powerful world of darkness the self had not previously known that was against everything good, true, and loving.

Everything God created was good. Good came first. *The only way evil can exist is to distort a positive created good.* Evil cannot exist independent of good, only in opposition to good. God created the human spirit with a will capable of going in either of two directions: one good, another, evil; one toward light, another toward darkness; either toward God, or away from God and toward Satan. God created humans with choice, so He put two trees in the garden, one the tree of Life, the other, the tree of the Knowledge of Good and Evil. But we don't just know about evil by what we choose. *Spiritually we become what we choose.* If we choose evil – we become evil. Spiritual darkness comes inside our being. But even when this darkness comes in we are not totally dark, or evil.

We don't like to think of human beings as having or being evil except in extreme circumstances. We avoid the harshness of the unbearable extreme

– thinking that we are evil instead of good. We would rather think of people as being good or bad.

But thinking about people as bad can be a distortion, as though some people can be defective. It implies that something is wrong with their created nature – the essence of their being or their being itself. Rather, there has been a twisting in our humanity. *"Evil" is the more accurate spiritual term to describe the misdirected use of our positive created resources.* To say that someone is "evil" is not to say that their essential being is beyond redemption, since they have not yet been totally destroyed. However, the total destruction of a person's being is the ultimate objective of evil.

Here's an illustration of what I'm trying to say. Battery acid is caustic but activates energy. In a battery, it can be put to good use. There are also evil uses to which battery acid can be put. That doesn't mean that there is something inherently wrong with the nature of battery acid itself. It is only the use to which it is put that makes it good or evil. In its proper use battery acid releases constructive energy. So it is with the self. With constant misuse there is a corruption and a corrosion of that essential nature, a bent toward evil and a misuse of our natures which were created for good. C.S. Lewis likes to describe the effects of evil on us as the "bentness" of our nature. Each human soul is either healed or damaged by the spirit with which it participates – the Spirit of light or spirit of darkness.

Hopefully, you can think of good and evil existing within each human being. The knowledge of evil within the self creates more than an image problem of how we see ourselves. It is important to understand how it has entered and affected our human nature.

Lonely Isolation: Knowing Who We Are Apart From God

This temptation in the garden was to know the self only as separated. The self knowing evil meant knowing only a self separated from God and all that expresses His character; knowing a self apart from the Truth, apart from Love, apart from Life, apart from Good, and even apart from the created goodness God created inherent in the self. This separation meant that we as humankind would have to learn who and what we are, apart from God.

In their loss of God-awareness, people became self-conscious. Their knowledge became completely self-centered. Even their knowledge which came in relationships became distorted because of self-interest. They were cut off from full consciousness of themselves, others and God. The knowledge of evil meant that the self would be cut off and isolated. The possibility of knowing the self only in its state cut off from God hadn't occurred to Adam and Eve. What a tragedy that they would choose to experience themselves in that way! They could now know themselves as separated, lonely, isolated, self-centered. Evil entered in, disconnecting them from God, creating heartbreaking anguish for each member of the human family to come. We could now know ourselves as being cut off from God, from others, and even from ourselves.

The legacy of this separation from the goodness of God and the goodness of the self means that we live with fears and doubts about ourselves. We carry guilt too, real guilt as well as imagined and false guilt. The struggle of many is the worry that in the essence of the self there is something defective, wrong, bad, contaminating, unlovable, unworthy, or terrible about our own core person, our innermost being. *Our worst fear is that even the best part about us, our love, is no good.* This deep fear is that our self-essence is not good for us or for others. This human tendency to question the self's created, essential goodness and frequent affirmations of the self's essential badness are explored further in a later chapter. Let me share some insights of how these things I'm talking about worked in my life.

MY PART

My father, who was a good man as well as a good father, nonetheless made a statement that proved to be one of the most powerful shaping forces in my life. He said to me, "Don't get your pleasure out of hurting other people." When he said that to me, I felt deeply hurt. I knew that wanting to hurt people wasn't my motivation. I was eight or nine years old at the time. "He doesn't know me," I thought. "He thinks I get into fights because I enjoy hurting people. He wouldn't say this to me unless he thought that I enjoyed hurting people." He was the person I most admired and respected in the world, so his opinion mattered a great deal to me. I interpreted his message to me as: "If you use your power to affect others, you will not be good for them; you will harm them."

I determined, in so far as it was possible, never to be guilty of using my power to affect another person in a way that wasn't good for him or her. Fear had entered my life. With it came distortions about myself. So, without even knowing I had made such a decision as a child, I organized a major part of my life around proving my father wrong about me. I began to create a false self. Not only could this self not hurt people, it could *not appear* to hurt people. This led to great difficulties in giving even normal corrective feedback to people. I was in my mid-thirties when I hired a couple of teen-age boys to paint our fence. They didn't have much experience at painting. I remember my frustration as I wanted to talk with them. I questioned myself, "If I say anything to them, would what I say be good for them?" I couldn't get myself to give them corrective feedback. But, at least, my difficulty surfaced. Then I could begin to shape ideas and words to describe to myself the problem I was having.

My unconscious motivation was to win back what I perceived as my father's lost approval. I created a self-idol, a perfect self that would never use my power to hurt people nor even appear to do so. During that time in my life, my life was more focused on my father's opinion of me than either my own or God's. An important part of my life was formed around defending against a false self. In directing my energy against disproving one false self, my father's wrong notion of me, I created another. Because of my fear of not being seen as good in my father's eyes, I inhibited the expression of power or leadership over others on the chance that I was wrong about myself, that I might not be good for others. I operated on the fear that if I used my power, it would not be for good; I would hurt someone else.

Let me draw some conclusions based on my experience. My fears illustrate how darkness enters a person. This fear created sin in me. Or, maybe I discovered sin that was already there through my fear. Something was wrong with me. Once there was something wrong with me, I needed to protect myself even from myself. *So, I created a positive, but false self to hide what's wrong in my unconscious while trying to appear fine to others.* My personal experience is a small picture of how our first parents yielded to temptation and sin created a false self in human personality.

Humanity needed a way to deal with what we wanted to know about ourselves, and what we didn't think we could stand to know. Defenses were formed to fill such an internal need. A positive or negative self-image is such a defense. These defenses functioned within the self as well as between the self and others. Defenses operate to hide things from both ourselves and others.

CREATED GOODNESS AND THE FALSE DEFENSIVE SELF

The only device that evil can use in the human spirit is to distort in an opposite direction the good that God created in the first place.

When sin entered into the human family, the ability to know things clearly and directly changed. The knowledge of evil meant a distortion in the knowledge of good. The destruction by corruption or distortion of a created good is the only option evil has to shape a human being. Evil has only one alternative regarding the human spirit – to take something essentially good that God has created and twist it into the opposite of good.

The correction is to acknowledge and turn from the evil we see in ourselves and reclaim the created gift that God gave us in the first place. Paul Hinnebusch, O.P., puts it this way. *"A person's faults are always closely related to his or her good tendencies and gifts because every fault is only a misuse of a God-given gift. Thus there is always a gift of God to be respected in the other person. My predominant weakness is closely related to my predominant strength."*[9]

This issue frequently comes up when I work with people with multiple personalities who have an alter, a separate personality or role as a part of the self, which identifies with evil and believes that he or she is essentially bad. With one woman, I talked with an alter whose role was protective in a defensive way. She said she was bad. Alters are usually formed in traumatic situations, sometimes with a demand on them to do something which is offensive or evil, which the person would not usually be willing to do. I assured her that before whatever life situation called her into being, God created her as good. If she had done evil as a child because someone required it or because she was trying to protect herself, there was something else in her, as well. God knew the person He created and what He designed her to be and that part of her spirit hadn't disappeared.

One of the ways in which she had protected herself was in dissociating feelings. *Not feeling* might better describe it. Or, put in a different way, she had "frozen feelings." I invited her to talk with Jesus about the way in which she saw herself and ask Him to show her how He saw her. She said that he began by showing her a small white flower on a mountain top, pushing its way up through the snow. He told her that she was like that flower. She protested that she couldn't be, that the flower was white and she was bad. Didn't He know the things she had done? He assured her that He knew about those things. These were things He had already forgiven her for – things that she had brought before Him as wrong. He then began singing the song "Eidelweiss" to her. Perhaps the reader knows the lyrics. "Blossom of snow you will bloom and grow, bloom and grow forever," and "clean and bright, pure and white, bless my homeland forever." These were some of the words that she said Jesus sang to her. She was overcome by the intimacy, the tenderness, the caring of His words and the meaning they carried.

"Blossom of snow" spoke to His knowing about her frozen emotions, and that He saw her as a flower, something beautiful that was awakening, and as white, someone who was now pure and clean, since she had confessed her sins and He had forgiven her. That she was going to bless His homeland of heaven forever filled her with gratitude. She knew how He treasured her. It didn't make sense to her why, but she knew it was true.

THE BIRTH OF THE UNCONSCIOUS

Sin against God created the unconscious, a darkness within the self. The formation of defenses occurred at the birth of the unconscious. One of the needs for an unconscious arose because of internalized rejection or a condemning self-judgment, the awareness that part or all of the self was unacceptable, either to someone outside ourselves at first, or later, to us. Our unconscious is brought into being to keep the knowledge hidden that a part of the self is unacceptable. Or it may serve the opposite role, to hide what is good about the self.

The people around us let us know what part of the self was acceptable, and what part was unacceptable. In some families and situations, the part of us that was good was acceptable, while the part of us that was not good was unacceptable. In other families and situations, only the part that was identified as bad or evil was acknowledged, while whatever was good in us was ignored or rejected. What is acceptable isn't often either good or bad, but is just a preference. Some people or cultures like people "plump." Others value "thin." Often, one is acceptable and the other is to be shunned.

So there were two alternatives which the unconscious had in viewing the self. People have the choice of becoming: 1) the good or perfect child or 2) the bad or rebellious child. There is, of course, an option that has nothing to do with the false self, 3) those who learn to view themselves accurately. In option one, things in us identified as evil or bad were driven into the unconscious, because we were allowed only to be good. Good alone was consciously allowed or expected of us. In option two, things identified as good were driven into the unconscious, and we were recognized or acknowledged only for the evil or bad. Evil or bad was expected of us and consciously allowed in our environment. Good had to be hidden. Healthy families, of course, are able to love children for all aspects of themselves and their behavior, even though they sometimes do things that are disliked.

UNCONSCIOUS CONFLICT

The unconscious is one way the self has of dealing with conflicts. Within us resides both a created good that is from God as well as that which is against God. What is against God is destructive to both ourselves and others. *Our hiding what is threatening or painful in the darkness of the unconscious is only a temporary solution left to the self once sin has entered into the world.* But now, we can invite Christ's love into our inner beings. When we do, His healing grace shines within us, dispelling darkness.

The unconscious may declare to the conscious self that everything is fine within the self when it isn't. For those whose conscious bias is, "I am good," it has a way of asserting, "I'm OK." But I may have gnawing doubts that something inside is wrong that I don't know about. In this case, the defensive position of self-distortion is that we consciously enhance the things we like about ourselves. We carry an image of ourselves that "I am good," and may deny anything in ourselves that doesn't fit with that view. In other words, we store all such information in our unconscious until we are in a climate of greater acceptance or love, so the disowned negative feelings can come to the light of consciousness. This posture is defensive in a self-enhancing direction. Self image and self-esteem are inflated in a positive, social approval direction.

Or the opposite may occur. The part of ourselves which we allow ourselves to know is the part that is not OK. We hide from ourselves and others that there could be a part of the self that is good, loving, beautiful, and lovely. This defensive posture is the "I am bad" posture – that there is nothing good in me. Guilt is the only truth. Condemnation of the self is the only position. Self-hatred is the defensive refuge. While self-hatred acts as a defense, it is none-the-less a powerful and destructive force that needs to be healed. This posture is defensive in a self-depreciating direction. Self-image and self-esteem are deflated in a negative, socially disapproved direction.

UNCONSCIOUS HIDING, A SEPARATION

When sin entered into the human family, a separation occurred between Adam and Eve and God, between each other, and within the self of each. The symptoms of this separation were fear, hiding, shame, and self-condemnation – or it's opposite, self-justification. When the Lord came to walk with them in the garden of Eden, they hid from Him among the trees. They displayed the separation already created within them from themselves by hiding from God. These first children of light now hid from the light of God's presence and from being in the presence of the Truth. Their consciousness was now split. Darkness had entered the light of their consciousness. They moved from enlightenment to self-deception. A split, a separation within the self, occurred as far as truth and self-knowledge were concerned. This unconscious split, this hiding of the self, was passed down to the entire human family. A contemporary person evidences this split by saying, "I think I spend most of my time living out the false self, and very little time in the true self."

Darkness involves hiding things we do not like about ourselves from ourselves, as well as from others. The job of the unconscious is to contain the truth which we do not like or which we reject in ourselves as threatening or painful. I believe that God created us with a bias toward growth and healing. As soon as the emotional climate warms us, our situation becomes less stressful. As we feel supported or accepted in significant ways, our unconscious begins presenting the hidden information to our conscious mind for emotional digestion and integration into consciousness. One role of the Holy Spirit within the self is to bring the truth to light. That is, to bring the things hidden in the darkness of the unconscious into the light of consciousness.

One of the ways in which the Holy Spirit is always at work in human personality is through dreaming. Our dreams reveal what we believe, what conflicts we have, what our strategies are for problem-solving, and where we are still stuck or trying to find solutions. That is one of the Holy Spirit's works, to reveal the truth to our conscious mind. The truth is hidden in symbols, the storage-language of the unconscious. As the symbols of the self come into the light of consciousness, the hiddenness continues until we are willing to discover the truth about ourselves. When we are ready, the symbols will yield their meaning. Thus the symbols in dreams hide and reveal at the same time; they are God's parables to mend the splits between the conscious mind and unconscious mind.

In The Openness Of The Spirit, Being Fully Known

Jesus' words used the metaphor of a lamp. Perhaps you can picture an ancient lamp with an oil wick lighted, burning brightly in a house. "Do you bring a lamp and put it under a bowl or a bed? Instead, don't you put it on its stand?" That way, it would illuminate everything around it. Then He continued, "For whatever is hidden is meant to be disclosed, and whatever is concealed is meant to be brought out into the open."[10] If the house is the self, the self is not made for concealment, but for the truth to come out into the light of consciousness. The spiritual principle is that hiddenness is the illusion.

Pain and suffering affect the very structure of the self. We put into the "deep storage" of the unconscious memories of threatening or painful experiences which we have not been able to know fully or process emotionally and mentally. So we take the conflict that distresses us and, using our defenses against it, we store a part of ourselves, the part of us that has had an indigestible painful or threatening experience. We have incorporated the very things we don't like into our psyche, along with our protective structures, our defenses against our feeling or remembering the experience. God's intent is that we approach the trouble hidden in us like the irritating grain of sand buried in the oyster. God transforms it into a treasure. First, we have to be willing to search for it.

These adaptive structures of the self need to be healed both by our openness to God and ourselves. Life is both an emotional and spiritual process. We, at some point, need to choose in favor of freedom for our spirit against the self-protective stance of not feeling our accumulated stored pain. Our defended-against past becomes our future until we're willing to experience our pain now in the presence of a loving and comforting God, friend, or helper.

Here's one story of healing through openness to God. Jenna had a rough childhood which included physical and sexual abuse. Later, she was in foster home settings. She experienced much rejection and created defenses against rejection. One of her defenses was "emotional numbing." One day she prayed for Jesus to remove all these defense barriers, and she said she heard in her spirit that her life would be different from now on.

The curse of defensiveness is its isolation. The Enemy of souls wants us to believe the lie that it will always be that way, that the truth is that we will always be alone. Jesus demolished that lie by bearing our griefs and carrying our sorrows.

Maggie's inner isolation makes her frightened of being alone. So, she's put great pressure on her husband to be with her and not go out on bicycle rides and leave her alone in the house. She does this because she is her own worst enemy. She's critical of herself. But guess what? He is too! The more dependency pressure she puts on him, the more critical he is of her. She needs to learn to nurture and care for herself as she would a friend or child. She can picture Jesus' love for her as a way for her to feel loved and valued, and so not alone. But she needs to begin treating herself that way too!

Nothing heals loneliness like experiencing our pain with someone who comforts us with their understanding, tears and hugs. Jesus' love makes Him willing to enter into our deepest need and pain and become our life-long Companion.

In the world of the spirit, all is open and known anyway. Every secret we keep from ourselves or others is openly known in the spiritual world. Every loved one who has died before us and is in heaven, along with every saint and all the heavenly hosts of angels are witnesses of all our earthly struggles as our allies. The book of Hebrews talks about this great cloud of witnesses we have in the spiritual world, and suggests therefore that we throw off every hindrance to our race of life, and every entangling sin, and fix our eyes on Jesus, Who has demonstrated how to perfect our faith in the middle of earthly struggles.[11] The writer to the Hebrews says the fact that all our secrets are known to a heavenly audience should motivate us to get rid of all our burdensome secret baggage, the sins that weigh us down with guilt and shame.

Here's how it worked for Jerry. After he prayed confessing childhood entanglements which he carried as god-like burdens, he declared: "I feel like a thousand pound concrete weight has been lifted off my shoulders!" A little bit of an exaggeration, but you get the point!

Returning to the metaphor of the lamp, Jesus said the eye is the lamp of the body. "When your eyes are good, your whole body is full of light. But when they are bad, your body is also full of darkness. See to it, then, that the light in you is not darkness. Therefore, if your whole body is full of light, and no part of it dark, it will be completely lighted, as when the light of a lamp shines on you."[12] The Apostle Paul talks about the light of consciousness when describing this earthly life and the future, heavenly spiritual life: "Now we see but a poor reflection as in a mirror: then we shall see face to face. Now I know in part; *then I shall know fully, even as I am fully known*.[13]

The eye is what guides our direction. *The mind's eye is the will*, which guides us. Our entire self – body, soul, and spirit – benefits from our good choices. We are also affected when we make choices that are part of darkness. Our unconscious carries not only the dark things others do to us, but also the unknown harm we inflict on ourselves with the unconscious choices we've made. The conscious mind is afflicted with a blindness, or a veil over it, when we participate in darkness. Then we lose a connection with ourselves, a complete knowing of ourselves. Into such darkness shines the inner light of conscience and the ever-present Light of the Holy Spirit. When God reveals us to ourselves, our knowing ourselves becomes complete and conscious.

---

1   Psalm 139:11-13

2   Psalm 139:1-10

3   Psalm 139: 23, 24

4   Lewis B. Smedes, *Love Within Limits*, Grand Rapids, MI: Wm. B. Eerdmans Publishing Co., 1978, p. 60.

5   Habakkuk 1:11 "… guilty men, whose own strength is their god."

6   Philippians 3:19 "Their destiny is destruction, their god is their stomach, and their glory is in their shame. Their mind is on earthly things."

7   Romans 5:8, 10 "But God demonstrates his own love for us in this: While we were still sinners, Christ died for us …. For if, when we were God's enemies, we were reconciled to him through the death of his son, how much more, having been reconciled, shall we be saved through his life!"

8   Jeremiah 29:13 "You will seek me and find me when you seek me with all your heart."

9   Paul Hinnebusch, *Spiritual Life*. "Anticipate one another in showing Honor," Vol. 42, No. 2, p. 70.

10   Mark 4:21, 22

11   Hebrews 12: 1, 2

12   Luke 11:34-36

13   1 Corinthians 13:12 (italics added).

Chapter 2

Restoring Worth

༃

*"My grace is sufficient for you, for my power is made
perfect in weakness," God told the Apostle Paul, who
responded: "Therefore I will boast all the more gladly
about my weaknesses, so that Christ's power may
rest on me. That is why, for Christ's sake, I delight in
weaknesses .... For when I am weak, then I am strong."*
2 Corinthians 12:9, 10

INTIMACY AND DEFENSES

Humility can restore our worth when we're willing to overcome the defensive barriers we've set up against intimacy.

We are created for intimacy with God and others. God eagerly awaits our friendship and companionship. But we put up barriers. Our defenses keep us distant not only from God, but from ourselves and others as well.

I'm going to take some time to describe defenses so you can recognize them and know how to deal with them. They're the way the self flexes its muscles. They represent a whole structure we build within ourselves to keep safe. Much represents the way we build a false self, which I described in the previous chapter.

Our eternal worth is at stake, in whether or not we exercise humility and overcome these relationship barriers that our defenses create.

VULNERABILITY: NEEDS, WEAKNESS

Some of us seem delighted to have weaknesses and exploit them. If so, we retreat from control defenses into impulsivity. Think about addictions as feeding appetites – eating, spending, sex, TV, alcohol, or drugs.

We may major on compliance solutions: passivity, approval seeking, and avoidance or withdrawal. Here, we're agreeable to a fault, hide out in our homes, or sleep a lot.

Maybe we're dependent. We may view our neediness as the ticket to get the care we want from others by needing things from them. Lots of time is spent on the phone or visiting.

In one set of defenses, people value control, or even aggression. In another, they prize the gratification and freedom of impulsivity. In a third, they seek withdrawal or taking the easy way.

You can't always trust the way people present themselves, either. Whether they present themselves in a positive or negative light, they may be faking it. On top of that, they probably don't know they're doing it.

Some of us exploit weaknesses in ourselves. If so, we retreat from control defenses into impulsivity, passivity, compliance, approval seeking and avoidance or withdrawal. If in the first, control is valued, here, gratification or taking the easy way is valued. Psychological tests have a defensiveness rating. People who hate weakness "fake positive." People who exploit weakness "fake negative."

Barriers Against Pain

Defenses are barriers we erect to contain emotional pain we have already experienced or which threaten us. Once we have an original experience with a person or in an environment, *we make predictions* about what is likely to occur in similar situations. Then we react or make decisions about what to do. *If these reactions are realistic, they are not defensive and create no problem. When they are defensive, our predictions distort the present situation.* Present realities often trigger past pain or threat. Defenses try to keep us from experiencing that past pain *now*.

Jeanna doesn't want to become part of a Christian community or develop adult friends because she fears the kind of rejection that came from her childhood. Defenses block us from experiencing ourselves fully because we may have lacked the ability to love, comfort and nurture ourselves when we're hurt. Defenses cut us off from intimacy with ourselves or others. Jeanna battles with self-criticism and self hatred, so she has difficulty experiencing rejection from others because she can't trust herself to be kind to herself. Life keeps providing opportunities to trigger past woundedness so we can heal. If we're willing, that is! It's extremely helpful if we understand that God is trying to heal us, not destroy us.

We need humility to overcome the defensive blocks in our ability to love ourselves or maintain an intimate relationship with others. Without this, we will not be able to maintain our feelings of personal worth. The problem with defensiveness is that it seems to be an assertion of our worth. Self-protection, even when defensive, seems self-validating. In the early self-esteem research by Coopersmith, he developed the observation that some people had "defensive high self-esteem." These are people who are sensitive to threats of loss of self-esteem and attempt to prevent the loss of self-esteem by defensive behavior or attitudes. This is not a plus for people. It describes a problem.

We all have a need for psychological protection. Such defensive needs affect not only our feelings of well-being, but our feelings of esteem as well. When our self-esteem is threatened, we are constantly tempted to abandon the vulnerability of humility (which can preserve intimacy) and resort to protective assertions of strength.

Clashing Defenses – The Personal Touch

My wife and I have a one room cottage behind our house. Once an in-law living-unit, it had recently been used for storage. Since it was cleared out, I went through it with a contractor friend so my wife and I could discuss remodeling plans. My assumption in remodeling is that we would rent it after we fixed it up. Late that night was the first time my wife Chris and I had had an opportunity to talk about it. Surprisingly to us, it quickly turned into a heated exchange.

"I work closely with people all the time!" Chris protested, raising her voice. "I don't want someone invading my space. My home is my haven where I can get away from people. I'm not ready to give that up!" It seemed to me that she reacted as though it were a done-deal and all the decisions had been made, as though I were about to sacrifice her solitude and end her privacy. "That's crazy!" I countered. "I just walked through the cottage to get some ideas. I was pleased to be able to solve so many of the problems."

Her intensity escalated. She said, "I know I'm overtired. I've been awake since four thirty this morning. Remember," she said, "the time we did have somebody staying out there? The noise came right up here – to our second story bedroom. I couldn't be talking like this in my own house because someone else would hear. That's what happened last time!" "That's crazy," I countered again. "We're not going to have the same kind of person living here again." Last time we had a high school student who had been kicked out of his home, who occasionally played loud music and had his friends over. It wasn't something that either of us would ever wish to repeat.

My viewpoint at the time was that I was trying to address her concerns and stay reasonable while trying to take a conflict-moderator role. Nothing I was saying was helping. Rather, the intensity kept escalating. I couldn't at the time see what I was doing that fanned the flames between us. Both of our defenses were being engaged. We both had some core vulnerabilities that were being triggered. In addition to the psychological climate, it seemed that there was some unseen force throwing gasoline on the fire. I suggested that we stop our discussion and pray for protection against any spiritual forces that might be attempting to escalate our conflict. It seemed remarkable to me that we had such a rapidly escalating disagreement after a serene evening in which I had been so aware of God's peaceful presence. So we prayed for God's help with the distress we were feeling, and trusted ourselves to God for His help in being able to meet our needs, as well as for God's protection in our relationship.

After prayer, we both felt calmer. Chris explained how she had felt when I said, "That's crazy." "I felt put in a corner and trapped," she said.

I began reflecting on how I was feeling. First, I became aware of some tension that I experienced as agitation. I was aware of some anger as a part of my agitation – a feeling of wanting to yell. I shared that feeling with Chris.

"Maybe you should have yelled," she suggested.

But more than anger, I felt sadness. "What was that about," I puzzled to myself? Our exchange had tapped into two areas of my unresolved emotional pain.

Cooling Down – A Time To Reflect

I began to try to understand my hidden motives. What had come up in our conflict that I hadn't been seeing in myself? First, I was feeling attacked, with no room being given for me or my opinions, my sense of not having a place to stand. Secondly, I was feeling that my motives to be considerate of Chris and my willingness not to do anything about remodeling that would cause her so much distress were being misunderstood. I realized then that my own feelings of being trapped came out in my comment, "That's crazy," and put her on the defensive. My comments created in Chris the feeling I was having, the feeling of being trapped. In my defensiveness, I had, unknown to me, created in her my trapped feeling.

I've described how our internal conflicts, needs, and defenses created an escalating tension in our relationship. The spiritual question is whether we were also under a spiritual assault? I wasn't sure, but it seemed likely. If so, then we had needed to use our spiritual resources as well, to help in resolution and healing.

Later, I remembered that I had prayed that morning that God would do His work in me that day in healing some of my unresolved issues from my family. That prayer certainly had been answered! I had some personal emotional work, some grieving to do before I would be able to get to sleep that night. I knew that beyond our temporary distress, God was uncovering in both Chris and me wounded, vulnerable feelings that needed healing and comfort. He was also wanting to heal and correct defensive adaptations with which we had learned to cope with our previous woundings.

What Are Defenses?

Defense implies a strategy of protection, like castles with drawbridges over moats, or forts built with thick walls. Much of psychology also uses the term "defenses" to refer to the positive roles of coping strategies, which are strategies of self-expression and life-management. In this chapter, I primarily use defenses to refer to coping strategies when they create distortions of present reality based on predictions we make based on past experience. Charlie had sent out graduation invitations and no one was responding. Even his mother had something else planned. He got angry and withdrawn. This fed into his previous rejected feelings. He didn't consider that his cell phone wasn't working and he hadn't been checking e-mails. Friends had actually tried to confirm the invitation, while he felt hurt.

Coping strategies are the strategic ways in which we interact with ourselves and our environments. The strategies are both conscious – those we know about – and unconscious – those we don't know about. The unconscious decisions come from earlier conscious vows we made and choices that were reactions we may not have been aware of. Everyone needs ways of interacting with both the personal and the physical environment. Such strategies begin before birth, since babies learn to find their thumbs or fingers to suck on while in the womb, which is probably a response to many different needs, including needs for comfort and security.

The Linns cite studies in which babies in the womb learn to respond to love and so adjust their position in the womb depending on where the love is originating outside the womb. A person would try to communicate love to the unborn baby while placing her or his hand on the abdomen of the pregnant mother. When a hand was placed on the right or left side of the abdomen, on the opposite side of where the fetus was positioned, the baby in the womb would change positions in order to be closer to the hand that was expressing love. Such studies indicate how responsive human beings are to love in their environment, even before birth, and develop coping strategies to respond to love.[1]

WHAT TRIGGERS DEFENSIVE REACTIONS?

When we react defensively, we respond to either of two triggers, pain or threat. Within this understanding of pain and threat, I am including the fear of losing positive feelings and the loss through frustration from delayed gratification. Pain and its damage or the fear of pain and its threatened damage are what trigger defensive reactions. We attempt to defend against the experience of pain or damage, or the anxiety, worry or fear that such damage will injure us in the future.

Many defenses deploy themselves instinctively without our thinking. Intellectualizing or rationalizing defenses do require thinking, even though the selection of that defensive reaction may not be a conscious choice. That is, the choice of what strategy to use in a given situation is often one we made long ago in decisions we've made, often in childhood. Our unconscious mind preselects the defense to fit the present circumstances based on associative similarities to past events and the success of certain defensive strategies in the past. Often, the original decision that set the defense in motion has been lost to conscious thought.

For example, Larry, as a young boy, was often beaten into helpless submission by his mother when he was between ages five and seven. He decided he would never let anyone get enough control over him to hurt him again. This set up an elaborate network of control defenses, compulsive in nature, that dominated his school life, and later, his work life, his friendships, how close he could let people be to him, and how he reacted to himself when he got hurt.

In later life when he was a manager, a woman whom he supervised, in a fit of temper, flung a file folder at him, hitting him in the shoulder. He was enraged inwardly. He felt violated, shamed, and humiliated. He felt angry and unforgiving of himself, as though he had somehow let this woman treat him in that way. He felt irrationally responsible for the way in which she had treated him abusively. His emotional and intellectual defensive reaction was that he was at fault for not doing whatever was necessary to keep himself from being hurt, hit, and humiliated.

He had, in fact, been violated and treated disrespectfully. But the intensity of his angry and helpless reaction did not come from this incident. Neither did his intense feelings of self-defeat and shame. His angry, controlling defenses drove him unmercifully. For no pain, hurt, or shame could be tolerated without its being his fault. He had made that choice long ago. His present emotional dilemma was acting out a script and a strategy from which he had not yet released himself. Not only was he at the time unable to forgive the woman who reported to him, but he was unable to forgive himself as well. As he continued to work his way through his mother's abuse of him, he came to the freedom within himself to be willing to forgive his mother. Had he been able to come to that forgiveness earlier and to complete his grieving about all the pain he experienced at his mother's hand, pain which he was helpless to prevent, he would have been able to respond with much less distress to his subordinate's outburst.

Are We Overreacting?

Spontaneity is the opposite of defensiveness. Experience that can be embraced entirely or in which we can express ourselves fully without fear can be processed fully in the moment. Experiences that have the potential for hurting us, evoking some memory of a past hurt, or threaten to damage us, call on our defenses to handle the situation. When we become aware that we are reacting defensively, we have the choice as to whether we will change our reactions.

Defenses are always appropriate in the presence of realistic danger. When the situation is realistically threatening, evasive or assertive action is appropriate. We are acting defensively, but it is appropriate. When we perceive the situation to be dangerous, but it is not, and we act defensively, we distort the reality of the present situation because of our past experience. We are really still reacting to the unprocessed pain from the past, and projecting it onto the present.

Ardis developed fear of contamination while using the bathroom. This led to elaborate, time consuming rituals of cleanliness. Why? Because her sister had to use the bathroom when she was in it, screamed at her and threatened to break the door down and hurt her. She knows now that her rituals are not based on present-day reality.

When we are defensive, we are unable to differentiate between past or present hurt without help from outside of ourselves. We need the feedback of an outside observer whose insight and relationship with us we can trust. If we've developed a good observer-self, we may be able to sort out the emotion of the moment and think through the situation at a later time.

Sometimes we know we're overreacting or are oversensitive. But we may not know why. At other times we may feel fully justified in our reactions, but they are unrealistic because we have not been able to distinguish between realistic present danger, and past, unprocessed pain and danger. Past danger that we have defended against, so we don't have to feel the pain, always gets projected on to new situations. It represents itself to our attention so we can be healed by recognizing our hurt and grieving about it.

I received a report from a property manager that felt intrusive and controlling. I was furious and stewed all that night. I didn't sleep well. I knew I was over-reacting. I valued figuring out what was getting triggered in me more than solving the situation. The next morning, as my wife Chris and I prayed, she got a picture of me at about age four when a carpenter threatened to "nail my shoes" to the porch. Chris could see me at this young age getting enraged because of this man's threat. Obviously, at that young age, I was in no position to express anger to that nasty workman. With the source revealed, the emotional power in the present situation evaporated. Later, I found that what triggered my reaction was only a misunderstanding.

Suppose we choose to become defensive again. We once again cut ourselves off from what is painful within us. The degree and intensity of our reaction may give us clues about whether we are overreacting, that is, whether we are reacting primarily to something that is not in the present situation. If a letter that someone sent made us react defensively, we might put it away and read it later when we're no longer distressed. Sometimes our distortions can be put aside, once the emotion of our initial reaction has passed and we are able to see clearly what felt threatening earlier.

INSIDE THE DEFENSES – HOW SELF-ABANDONMENT CAN HAPPEN

The internal goal of defenses is to force painful, hurt, or threatening feelings out of consciousness until our internal and external environments make it safe for us to experience them. The temporary defensive strategy of the unconscious is to keep all unwanted feelings outside of awareness. How? We control, squash, deny, dissociate or eliminate such thoughts, memories, or beliefs about the self. But, once we're willing and able to accept our undesirable areas, we're ready to begin the spiritual and emotional process of healing.

The original objective of defenses was to protect us from pain, harm, or threat from our environment. However, the drama between us and our environment gets reenacted and brought inside us too. We once wanted to keep others from hurting us. Now, pain we have already experienced we try to defend against within ourselves. We try to prevent ourselves from knowing about or having an awareness of painful feelings which we have already experienced. So we hurt ourselves with our defenses to keep from knowing previous pain.

We can create *substitute pain*. The substitute is not supposed to be as bad as the original pain and gives an alternate focus. Intentional burning or cutting oneself is often done with this purpose.

Defenses can be applied force. When we direct them against ourselves, we hurt ourselves again. Defenses of *repression* are the sledge hammer of force. Defenses of *dissociation* are the scissors which snip experience from one place and paste it somewhere else, where it won't be recognized or found easily.

Stephanie tried to suppress current emotional pain. She had a dream about being in prison (the structure of her defenses). In prison, water (emotions and painful feelings) kept rising, flooding the room. She tried frantically to rearrange the furniture to keep above the tide, but eventually the water covered every dry surface. She panicked because she couldn't escape the water and feared drowning in it. The interpretation? She was overwhelmed by feeling her pain. It was unavoidable. Yet she feared that her life, as she knew it, was about to end.

Defenses are utilized when a person experiences hurt, pain, or threat that the person is unable to respond to fully at the time. The painful or threatening feeling will be stored in an encapsulated form in memory. Sometimes, if the memory includes pain inflicted on our bodies, or threat connected with a particular bodily location, it will be stored as a body-memory.

A destructive situation which somebody cannot prevent happening creates secondary reactions. Those secondary reactions have to do with beliefs, the ways in which we interpret our experiences and our emotional reactions to them, and how we position ourselves and our feelings regarding our experiences. The objective in using a defense is often to contain the event, to encapsulate and isolate the thoughts and the emotions connected with the experience. This defensive approach is used if the internal environment of the self or the external environment of others makes it unsafe to process the experience. If such safety or trust does exist, then defensive containment is necessary only to the degree to which the experience cannot be fully processed at the present time.

Feelings of helplessness are often present when a loss of control occurs and we can't stop something from happening that damages us. People often hold themselves responsible for such injuries by telling themselves they should have been able to protect themselves. Often this position is unrealistic, and the belief is held irrationally. When we do this, we engage in this secondary self-inflicted trauma because we feel so vulnerable, hurt, emotionally devastated and perhaps panic stricken that anything feels better than acknowledging and feeling our weakness and helplessness. When this secondary reaction to our pain and helplessness occurs, another control layer of the self has been added to the defense structure through our aggression against ourselves.

Originally, someone else was against us. Now the self turns against the self. In the service of self-protection, we become enemies of ourselves. What happens in a situation of threat is that the self is actually defending against painful feelings the we have already experienced. We are not just protecting ourselves from the present situation. *When we defend ourselves by being hard on ourselves, a self-abandonment occurs under the guise of self-protection.* One person attempted to make fun of this process in himself by saying, "After tennis, beating up on myself is my favorite sport."

THE ABILITY TO BE AGAINST OURSELVES

Defenses occur against others or against the self. Many kinds of defenses are possible. I'm emphasizing two primary types: 1) assertive defenses, which can also be aggressive, and 2) withdrawing, avoidant defenses. Intellectual control or cognitive processes, such as thinking, rationalizing, and analyzing, can be used not only to cope with the situation, but as a withdrawing defense. If we use our thinking processes to guide us away from our emotional reactions, it may have a function of pain avoidance. Dissociative defenses may be used to split off both assertive and withdrawing reactions.

Either through a genetic predisposition or because of learned experience, people learn to use the defense that is most successful for them. It may be a defense style that is allowed, encouraged or not heavily punished by parents. One father angrily yells at his son whenever the son starts explaining himself. Why? It's the father's own favorite defense, one which he is unconsciously angry at himself for needing and using. He can see the anger he feels at himself getting dumped on his son. Hopefully, he'll draw that conclusion and change how he treats both his son and himself.

Children experiment with testing the limits with their parents very early in life. They learn what works best with each parent. They begin constructing an elaborate set of predictions to explain the ways in which their parents react to them, and in what situations to expect which parental behavior. Children are naturally expressive of their wishes and needs. The strategies of expression may be assertive, if they want something, or withdrawing, if they want to avoid something.

As soon as children learn that they can act for or against themselves, they can begin to develop the defensive role of being against the self. These inner defenses, I believe, are designed to protect the core of the self, the true self. Of the two defenses, either aggressive or withdrawing, the ones that are most noticeable are aggressive defenses. Passive defenses against the self are easier to overlook. Sleeping more than needed, watching too much television, reading to escape, delaying getting things done, and being indecisive are easier to slip by without being noticed.

Aggressive defenses are usually formed in the presence of a misuse of power. When a person experiences someone who is aggressive against him among the persons who are close to him or have power over him, he can internalize the role of that person as an aggressor and become, by identification, an aggressor against himself. With that internalization, he can anticipate how he'll be treated in the outside world by knowing how the person who is close to him harms him. Then he can do it to himself first. It feels to some people that if they hurt themselves first, it protects them. They have control. They might keep outside harm from coming if they act against themselves first. It often seems that it hurts less if the self does the injury than if someone else does it. People who have multiple personalities routinely have *alters*, that is self roles, or personalities whose function it is to be protective, who learned to be against the self. These are often called "aggressive alters;" it is understood that their function is to protect the self.

Of course, when the self is against the self, this creates a problem. If it is the self that is doing the injury, it is the self against the self. Then there's no one to stop the damage. What started out as a strategy for self-protection, which often was considered necessary for survival or pain-avoidance, now is a self-destructive cycle. The cycle often seems out of control. Such cycles often cannot be seen, let alone corrected, without outside intervention. The problem with such self-directed violence is that we suppress pain only with greater force than the original pain. Therefore, we are burdening ourselves with greater pain by what we do to ourselves. To be able to carry that pain, and continue to suppress it, we have to stay angry or get angry with ourselves whenever the area of our unconscious pain or threat is triggered.

Symptoms – Protections Which Both Hide Us And Reveal Us

In order to learn to respect ourselves and honor others, we need to learn how defenses work. Hiding and revealing are simultaneous and paradoxical goals of defenses. These defenses display themselves as symptoms. Protection is one primary goal of our defenses. The first objective is to hide from others the things they might use to hurt us. One way to hide things from others is to hide them from ourselves so we don't know what the unwanted truth about ourselves is. The logic of the unconscious is that if we don't know something or have something – that is, it's hidden from us – then we are better able to protect ourselves from being hurt by others. Not knowing gives us "plausible deniability," so we can act as though certain things aren't true of us.

There's a dilemma in hiding information from ourselves. Fear escalates when something is wrong and we don't know what it is. It's as if alarm bells and flashing lights went off in the psyche. The solution for fear is to turn the light switch on in the dark room of our consciousness. When we see what bothers us, in most cases, we'll be better able to cope with it. The problem is that we need to be willing to experience the painful feelings we have been hiding from ourselves. *The ability to grieve and process pain is an essential emotional skill in relinquishing fear and confronting the truth about ourselves.*

Defenses also reveal. The unresolved need or conflict we have is hidden like a puzzle in every defense. What is hidden from us is often clear to others. That's why loving, truthful friends or therapists who are trained to understand how the defenses work can help unravel these mysteries.

I have often seen people who don't like something about themselves produce a symptom that is unacceptable to them; overweight, smoking, being late, an unwanted behavior. One way in which this can play itself out is for the symptom to get focused outwardly in relationships as something that the spouse or friend has to change his or her attitude about. The push is for acceptance of the person the way he or she is, with his or her symptom.

Why? Because the symptom symbolizes some way in which they have been rejected and something they reject in themselves. So they have no hope of changing the behavior or feeling by themselves. Unconscious sabotage asserts itself as a demand for the symptom to be accepted by someone outside the self as a symbolic unconditional acceptance of the person. So people cling to their symptoms with an almost desperate defiance. Meanwhile, the core problem of self-rejection is not seen, while blame shifts away from the self to someone outside the self.

If there is something about us that makes us utterly unacceptable to ourselves or to someone else who is important to us, we will often feel a need to act out our internal conflict and identify with that rejected part of ourselves with the unconscious hope of resolving our rejection feelings.

The defensive symptom we pick serves two functions. One function would be to reveal our self-rejection while enacting a defense against something rejecting, such as criticism. It puts our problem on display so that we cannot ignore it. We have to keep facing it. Sometimes there is so much anger attached to being rejected that there is an unconscious wish to declare forcefully that it is not right to have your whole person judged and rejected based on a single value or behavior. Mark's symptom illustrates these two functions. He occasionally tramples his boundaries in watching TV past midnight. This act rebels against his perfectionism. But it broadcasts his problem in not accepting himself. Also, he can't hide his tiredness from himself or others, so his rebellion is likely to be discovered. When we love and accept ourselves the way we are, we create the climate in which change can occur. The same is true of relationships.

Jennifer, a bright, interesting, creative woman is in love with Rodney, an artistically talented man. They are friends. It could be a great deal more than that because they both love each other. There is one problem: her weight. In terms of attraction, he's turned off sexually by her "fat." So, they remain friends, but he gets involved with someone else to whom he is attracted. He doesn't love this person. He hopes she'll love him though, but he doesn't expect it.

They both operate with defenses that prevent themselves from getting what they most want. Jennifer says of herself and her weight, "that's just the way I am." While not all people with weight problems are defensive, let's assume that she is. What could be the problem? A lack of nurture leads some to eat "comfort food." If her emotional neediness is great, and food serves as a primary resource for meeting those needs, it will show. The defense chosen reveals the need. So the need for emotional nurture is hidden, but it shows up in symbolic form, body weight.

Some people get unwanted sexual attention before they're ready for it, or worse yet, are sexually abused and so develop a negative attitude toward their bodies and physical attractiveness. Fat can provide layers of protection against unwanted attention. Then, in a relationship, a person can become demanding that the other person accept him or her unconditionally, with his or her weight. Such a demand puts the issue of rejection or abuse into the relationship that the person has not yet been willing or able to face.

Rejection Dynamic

The rejection dynamic which Jennifer could express through her weight might go like this. "My issue is rejection. I'm angry about the rejection I've received. So I require of my friends that they pass my test of whether I can trust them. If they like me and love me regardless of what I look like, I think they can like me for who I am as a person, not for what I can do for them." Notice that because she has not been able to respond to her needs for acceptance with anything but rejection, she cannot respond to his wishes for her to look different in an accepting way either.

Rodney came to the conclusion through his experiences that he would not be loved or valued by a woman, so he didn't expect a woman to commit to a relationship with him. He allowed himself to become attached to someone who was not capable of or willing to return his affection. He let himself be used. He didn't expect any more for himself. He pursued relationships where women would reject him and were not willing to make commitments to him. He offered himself to people who were not capable of offering themselves to him.

Because he defends against rejection and potential loss by low expectations – hoping for little for himself, he has experienced the pain of rejection after rejection. When he doesn't get love, the pain of rejection is minimized, because he has gotten what he expected. He sells himself short. He is willing to get into relationships with people he doesn't love, because he doesn't feel he deserves to have someone love him, nor to have someone he loves. With these two people, we see that people use defense styles that fit their personality styles which are developed in their own life experiences.

CONDITIONING AND DEFENSES

Panic disorders and phobias are defenses in which conditioned memories of painful experiences evoke fear, triggering an avoidance response or panic. In a phobia, the fear gets transferred and attached to a stimulus situation or external object. I had one such phobic response after I experienced a painful firing from the church I started. In the first few years after our family moved out of the area, when I came back for a visit, as I saw the city limits sign as I drove into the city where I had worked, I noticed myself experiencing a fear response. My fear response attached to the city limits sign meant that I had undigested emotional pain.

Another example illustrates how phobic attachments are formed. A woman could not get herself to cross a bridge across the bay to another city, because there are no exits on the bridge. When she couldn't get off a bridge once she's on it, panic set in. Why? Because it is like the loss of control she felt while growing up. She had an angry father who criticized and belittled her. She couldn't control the situation. She had to contain the hurt and not show it. Super-control over her emotions was necessary for the sake of survival so she did not show her vulnerability and hand over more power to her father who attacked her. Anxious perfectionistic control became her ally.

Going over the bridge was like handing over control to her father. She felt that the control moved from inside her to outside her. The bridge felt like something that exerted control over her from the outside. Crossing the bridge evoked panic at the feared loss of control. Avoiding crossing the bridge was in reality avoiding the painful and helpless feelings over her inability to control what hurt her in the past, which pain was still present with her.

Anxiety or fear in the form of panic defends against pain. Terror can do the same thing. Terror evoked by a painful traumatic memory can be the fear of pain. A stimulus trigger can come from any thing in present day life which was associated with the original trauma. A person who sees a commercial for dog food on television in which the dog in the ad is like the one who bit him as a child could experience an immediate terrified feeling while watching the ad, if the original fright and pain is still unprocessed and stored in the memory-bank of the unconscious.

The fear of fear, the fear of anger, the fear of pain and the fear of feelings motivate panic. The fear of pain often motivates anger and self-directed abuse. These are secondary responses to an experience. First, we have an experience. Second, we take a position regarding the experience. In panic, we take a "flight response." We vacate our wounded self. We flee – or attempt to flee – the feelings of our experience. In anger, we take the "fight response" to the feelings of our experience. In either position, the self is against the self: one by withdrawing, one by aggression.

HONOR, ESTEEM AND DEFENSES

When we perpetuate our defenses against ourselves by being hard on ourselves we continue the reenactment of rejection by a self-rejection. In doing this, we dishonor ourselves. Sirach writes: "My child, with humility, have self-esteem and value yourself at your proper worth. Who will justify the person who sins against self? Who will honor the person who dishonors his own life?"[2] When we through defensive and self-inflicted rejection dishonor ourselves, we also dishonor the loving death of Jesus on our behalf, Who died for this very reason, to free us from the bondage of that self-inflicted death. To become free of our need for defensiveness, we must be open to receiving His love and help in the places where we're presently defensive and wounded, in the very places in which we cannot help ourselves.

Honor should be given not just to ourselves through non-defensiveness, but to others as well. Our love will not create defensive barriers between ourselves and others. The Apostle Paul instructs, "Love must be sincere."[3] To love with sincerity means to love non-defensively. Positively, that means not just giving others the impression of loving them but being truly loving. We also attempt to avoid dishonoring others by treating them defensively. Even when we realistically need to take defensive action with someone, it should not be in a way that is against her or him, but in such a way that is respectful of both the other person and of ourselves. "Do not repay anyone evil for evil …. If it is possible, as far as it depends on you, live at peace with everyone."[4] After telling us to be devoted to one another in brotherly and sisterly affection, he continues, "take delight in honoring each other."[5]

Honor is the outward display of inward esteem for the other person. "What does it mean to honor someone?" asks Paul Hinnebusch. "First, the recognition of the other person's dignity and worth; second, a loving appreciation and approval of this worth, an esteem for this value which we recognize in the other; third, a sign expressing this esteem, a mark of appreciation and approval. Honor is not honor until reverence and esteem for the other are shown in some practical way."[6]

He further talks about the transforming glory of God which changes people as God's life penetrates them more and more. "It is my responsibility to encourage that transformation by the reverence and honor I show that person. When I show honest esteem for another person by the way I treat him, I beget a healthy self-esteem in him. My reverence for him calls forth from his heart a holy reverence for himself. If he has no self-esteem, it is probably because others have not treated him with esteem. If he does not esteem himself, he will not live in keeping with his dignity and worth as a son or daughter of God."[7]

"True love," he says, "does everything it can to promote the dignity and self-esteem of the loved one. Anytime I manipulate another person for my own advantage, I dishonor the person I so use and thereby dishonor his Father in heaven." Further he says, "Love in response to love is the fullness of God's image in us. God's image in us has not reached its full glory till we are full of love for others as the Father is for the Son, and the Son is for the Father in the Holy Spirit of love."[8] The fullness of God's love in us means that we can love our enemies and treat them with respect, even when they are against us and don't treat us with respect.

SELF-ACCEPTANCE IS THE OPPOSITE OF DEFENSIVENESS

Loving ourselves, forgiving ourselves and liking ourselves deals a death blow to the defensiveness that rejects the self and damages intimacy with God and others. Accepting our own weakness or vulnerability without judging ourselves for our inadequacy is a first step away from defensiveness. It is then that we can welcome the power of God's love which can become our strength. Receiving the inner springs of His love through His Spirit enables that life-flow first to come into us to heal us and then pass through us to others. God's love within us is sufficient to heal the internalized enemy within – which creates our defensive barriers – and participate in the healing of those outside ourselves who may be against us, offering them something they aren't expecting. Love testifies to hostility that there is another way. Honor greets mistreatment and esteem responds to being demeaned. We can begin to create a new emotional and spiritual climate, giving the person who has been against us an awareness of a new option: to be loving and retain feelings of worth in the presence of opposition or attack.

Through God's powerful love within us, we have a greater energy than any defensive force we might muster to keep ourselves safe and protected. *Love is infinitely greater than defenses based on fear.* We are no longer able to be dominated by our environment and forced by our fear of its power into becoming reactive. When Love so captures us, we will not lose our worth when we are tempted to react fearfully. If we do stumble and fall, we will get up and return to our Father, confessing our failings. We will act as sons and daughters of our heavenly Father, not as children of the world, realizing that greater is He that is in us than he that is in the world.[9]

We will not be able to respond with love to others when they inflict pain unless we have first been willing to love ourselves by grieving through the pain we have already experienced. God in His love eagerly assists us in our growth into the fullness of love and out of the weakness of our defensiveness – our temporary human strength.

Reality tests our defenses. Those which are not skills and coping strategies, but self-protective distortions must be broken down by life experiences or melted with kindness so we do not cling to their false strength. Such false strength is a self idol[10] which God is eager to have us replace with trust in Himself. *Hardship and adversity break down the faulty strength we erect to handle difficulties so we will not cling to worthless idols and so become worthless ourselves.*[11] God's gracious loving kindness, forgiveness and mercy let us know we can fully trust in His restorative love. He has created us to be His masterpiece and what life mars, He restores.[12] We can be confident that He who has begun a good work in us will complete it by the time Jesus comes again.[13]

1 Dennis Linn, Sheila Fabricant Linn and Matthew Linn, *Healing the Eight Stages of Life*, audio tape # 1

2 Sirach 10:27, 28 (Translation in Hinnebusch, *Ibid.*, p. 69)

3 Romans 10:9

4 Romans 12:16

5 Romans 12:10, TLB

6 Hinnebusch, *Ibid.*, p. 67

7 *Ibid.*, p. 70

8 *Ibid.*, p. 70

9 1 John 4:4

10 Habakkuk 1:11 "... guilty men whose own strength is their god."

11 Jeremiah 2:5 "This is what the LORD says: 'What fault did your fathers find in me, that they strayed so far from me? They followed worthless idols and became worthless themselves.'"

12 Ephesians 2:10 "For we are God's workmanship created in Christ Jesus to do good works, which God has prepared in advance for us to do."

13 Philippians 1:6

Chapter 3

When Love Hurts

జ౧

"How precious concerning me are Your thoughts, O
God! How vast is the sum of them! Were I to count them,
they would outnumber the grains of sand.
When I awake, I am still with You."
Psalm 139:17, 18 [personal translation]

THE PAIN IN LOVE

Sometimes, love can be a real pain. It takes a surrendering to love if we're going to heal our defensiveness. When we have been hurt or our trust betrayed by previous blows, love can trigger intense emotional pain.

Belinda wrestles with continuing in therapy and in her connection with two special friends. Why? Because she is beginning to trust them and it frightens her. She's feeling more emotional pain than she ever has and her sadness perpetually lurks beneath the surface. She understands the truth that she's never trusted a single soul. Now she's found friends that she knows she can trust. But she doesn't feel safe and she can barely get herself to draw on the small strands of trust that bind her to her friends because she fears being flooded and overwhelmed by all the pain she's never let herself feel.

Loving her friends and feeling their love compels her to keep trying to develop new levels of trust, but it also exposes a new rawness of hidden emotional pain. She knows that if she bails out on her friendships, she'll never feel the love and closeness to God she's desperate for. You can see her dilemma. Her defenses want her to close down to avoid pain. Her love and the love of others force her to choose between the safety of the pain she wants to avoid and slugging her way through what feels unbearable to remove the blocks to intimacy her defenses put up.

If it's hard for us to trust and receive love from others, we will likely have difficulty loving ourselves as well. That means we will tend to use defensive ways of handling our own pain. Our willingness to heal defensiveness means we need to be willing to take in love from others as well as give love to ourselves. Developing self-nurture skills is an antidote to previously poisonous relationships. We need kindness and caring from ourselves or others if we are pained or distressed. This comfort can keep us from feeling isolated, lonely, and perhaps, bitter. If we treat our emotional pain defensively, we set ourselves up for internal alienation and feelings of loneliness. Then we won't accomplish God's intention. He wants to heal us with the past we've had.

Putting God in the picture can make people bristle when they blame Him for their suffering. A sovereign God who allows suffering sometimes makes people angry. But God gives people free will which puts boundaries around how He exercises His sovereignty. Actually, He designed life with His willingness to enter into and share every bit of pain we experience. "Surely our griefs He Himself bore, And our sorrows He carried ...."[1]

He does nothing to short-circuit free will. He wants our love of Him to be entirely voluntary. But God's carrying our sorrow through Jesus means that He has entered into every bit of isolation and abandonment that has pained us. Pain often triggers the fear of loneliness which creates one of our biggest obstacles in our willingness to heal. Let me assure you that God intimately knows everything about us, His presence is always with us, and He unfailingly wills our emotional and spiritual healing.

Now for our part. It takes humility to overcome defensiveness, to be willing to experience our emotional pain without trouncing ourselves, blaming others, retreating into the fog of self-numbing through food, activity, sleep or other aggressive or withdrawing addictive habits. The defensiveness which needs healing is our tendency to act self-protectively when it isn't necessary, when there isn't a real external threat. Defensiveness also deals with hidden pain we try to block from ourselves so we don't feel it. Defenses are needed coping strategies; but defensiveness walls us off from intimacy with ourselves and others. It takes telling ourselves the truth about what caused the pain and not sending in the storm troops of self-berating, negative predictions, confusion, or criticism of others to rescue us from what hurts us.

Martha had so much trauma in her younger life that she often preferred to go into her room and keep the shades pulled and stay in darkness where no one could bother her. She recently made a decision to surrender to God all the critical areas of her life, her trauma, her feelings about her abuser, her feelings about her body, and her wish to die. This release to God brought the most significant change in her life in two years of therapy, because she was willing to heal her pain rather than willing to resist it with all her might – her defenses. She began waking up with a peaceful calm, rather than wondering why she was alive and wishing she were dead.

Defenses are formed as one way of dealing with emotional pain. Grieving is another alternative. The strength to grieve comes from the comfort of love. It is a great comfort to know that God knows us intimately and loves us unconditionally with great compassion in our sorrow. There is nothing concerning us about which He has not already thought. There is nothing we are interested in concerning ourselves about which He is not infinitely more concerned for us than we are for ourselves. He is present with us in our hardships as One Who has immersed Himself in our lives. He leads us to joy through our mourning. It seems to me that the greatest pain is the dark, despairing loneliness of believing that God is not available to help, is not interested, is not present with us. Then we are left with only ourselves and our sometimes brutal devices to blot out the awareness of our distresses.

TOUGH TACTICS

Defenses within the self are structured in a priority of what works. One approach is the use of intellectual – or thinking – defenses to attempt to control emotional reactions. Other defenses can be used to exert control. Anger as a control defense may be focused on someone else, maybe blaming or criticizing him or her. As long as we stay angry, we stifle the awareness that we feel hurt. Sometimes, if people cannot sustain anger at others, they become angry at themselves. Unmerciful, self-inflicted beatings can occur. Usually, these are verbal and mental beatings. "How could you be so dumb? Where were you when brains were passed out?" "You're a coward and a wimp!" "You don't deserve the air you breathe." "Crybaby! You're just having a pity party." Tough and hurtful talk!

When I hear this verbal hammering I can picture a smaller person trying to talk, think, express needs, cry, or feel hurt in the presence of an overbearing "tough guy." These verbal beatings are like a bully trying to intimidate a vulnerable person into silence by toughness, ridicule or shame. Sometimes the beatings are even physical and self-inflicted – whatever works in the arsenal of defenses. The bully-self pulls out a bigger weapon and uses it against the emotional-self, sometimes the smaller, childlike, weaker – that is, more vulnerable – self, attempting to silence it. So you'll understand and not be critical of such a person, the internalized "tough-guy" is an aggressive defender of the self because there was such a harsh person in his or her life. Such defensive anger attempts to cover over pain and fear or dissociate it. I have seen an adult woman slam her fist full force into a wood post. The physical pain had its desired impact. It drove the more vulnerable emotional pain out of consciousness. Self-inflicted cutting or cigarette burns have a similar numbing dissociative effect.

If not anger, anxiety or fear may be the predominant covering or controlling emotion of defense. The fear of pain may drive us away from pain through avoidance defenses. Some people with a lot of unprocessed pain often fear tapping into that emotional pool, for fear of being overwhelmed with the grief or sorrow being stored outside of consciousness. There are other reasons for the fear. Perhaps these people never learned that their negative feelings were acceptable. Maybe they were shamed when they cried so they learned to be frightened of shame and so avoid painful feelings that bring on tears.

In the use of controlling emotions like anger, fear, and anxiety in the service of defense, a redirection is necessary. Whether it's rationalizing, obsessive worrying, demeaning self-talk, or self-beatings, a decision must be made to stop the defensive responses and to be willing to experience the sadness, threat, pain, or sometimes anger that is beneath.

LOVE SETS US FREE FROM DEFENSIVENESS

Love is part of the truth that sets us free. God spoke a clear message to one person for her overweight friend. She conveyed it to her friend. "God loves you as you are. He does not want to change you. He wants you to know how much He loves you and for you to accept His love." When she heard this, she wanted to get off the phone and have an alcoholic drink, something to numb her. Her friend said, "Why don't you pray instead. God misses you. He wants to be with you. He experiences pain if you pull away from Him." She let her friend know that the choice was hers.

Humility is required of us to understand and accept ourselves the way we are and to be willing to receive the love we need. As we notice that we are different from the way we'd like to be, it is important to rest in God and in His loving acceptance of us as we are now. God accepts us in the most troublesome areas of our weakness.

The irony is this. Our own acceptance of the things we reject in ourselves is the very thing that makes lasting change possible. In order to change and heal, we must first come to an ownership of the defensive part of our self which we'd like to ignore or reject. We typically see these as symptoms, complaints, weaknesses, or burdens, and may have a hard time coming to an ownership of the truth that, at least unconsciously, we have chosen this particular symptom which we may hate in ourselves and have not yet been ready to give it up.

TAKING OWNERSHIP

I talked earlier about my own struggles with administrative management. When Jesus let me know of His love for me and asked me to follow Him without making my failures such a focus of my attention, there was something else He let me know. He wanted me to know that the struggle I had was the way I had wanted things; that I needed to see how my choice of this symptom served what I wanted. The struggle and the effort was so great, it stunned me at first to think that I was choosing this. Emotionally, it was hard for me to see how that could be possible. But knowing how defenses work and the need for ownership in order to change, I began to search to find out what I truly wanted and was choosing for myself.

Taking ownership of the defensive part of ourselves that creates misery and distress and which we often fight to control is not easy to embrace or to see. Henry prays daily that God will help him with his self-control.

His emotional outbursts, even though reduced to only once every couple of months, have created tension with his wife and stressed his staff. He described Tuesday as one of the worst days he's had emotionally in a long time. He wanted to take a chair and throw it on the ground and crumple it. "I felt a need to break something," he said. "If I didn't break something, something would break me." So he took his glasses off and threw them against the partition and broke the frames. He hadn't had them fixed as a way of punishing himself, reminding himself, "This is what you get for losing control." He said, "I feel like I'm trapped, like I'm in a box or cage I can't get out of."

What led up to this? He had forgotten to do something and a client was counting on him. He could not tolerate his mistake of forgetting so he got furious with himself. Why? He felt helpless. He needed to ask someone for some help, but he did not feel valuable enough to ask someone. He told himself, "You don't have the right to ask for help. Your father wouldn't ask for help. You can't, either!" He was stuck. I asked him what effect his outburst had on his feelings of helplessness. He said he gets help without having to ask. To enable him to take ownership of his defensive feelings, I tried to put his position into words. "My feelings of being a competent person are based on my being a person like my father who I thought could do things without ever asking for help. I view feeling helpless as a failure that makes me look stupid, feel foolish, silly and incompetent. I am willing to do anything – including having outbursts – not to break, and admit that I'm helpless and need help."

In our distress, we usually think of our defenses as outside of our control. When we take ownership of a defensive feeling or behavior and see what we're getting out of it and that it is within our control, we have the power to decide to change it. We do not have that power as long as we think of ourselves as struggling against something which is outside of our control. We also come into a position of being able to ask God's help both to accept and to forgive ourselves, as well as to change.

Once we take God's love and acceptance into ourselves, we have new options as to how to be. We learn we have new freedoms. Earlier, I talked about protective weight. But other defenses could be: being aggressive, negative, disagreeable, pessimistic, expecting the worst, complaining, angry, shy, or withdrawn. (I saw a picture of one of these in action. A person wore a tee shirt with the bold message, "Don't bother me!") Here are some positive sounding defenses that may surprise you: being a "bubbly personality," being good, or being a "nice" person.

God has no difficulty accepting us. God expressed His love toward us while we were still sinners, while we were His enemies and against Him and against ourselves. He did not require that we change in any way in order for us to be loved.[2] The defensive self we carry around is our rejected self. That is who we are before accepting and loving ourselves and before coming to God for His love. We need to understand that even while we are defensive we are loved by God. We don't have to be different or change to become worthy of God's love, to earn it or to have Him accept us. We who believe in God's unconditional love have the greatest resource possible to know and love ourselves, to forgive and accept ourselves exactly the way we are. Then we can grow into the freedom of sons and daughters of the Most High.

INTIMACY HEALS DEFENSIVENESS

What does it take for us to become open to healing when we are defensive? We need to acknowledge what the truth is about ourselves. We need to be willing to let our barriers down, between us and God, between us and ourselves, and between ourselves and others. We need to be willing to take in another's loving presence. Often we're unwilling to do that, because we know, at least at an unconscious level, that to open ourselves to love also opens the door to the pain we have not yet processed.

Experiencing the positive feelings of love, attachment, being liked, and knowing that you matter to someone, rebuilds trust. It also opens the associative pathways to where our pain is stored if we've been hurt by someone whom we've cared about. Our present experience of love can open past pain from our woundedness. Some people defensively shut the door on that pain by sabotaging intimacy and re-creating relationships where emotional distance and defensiveness are needed. People often choose, whether consciously or unconsciously, to defend against experiencing their previous pain by avoiding intimacy in the present. They do it not only with friends, but with God.

God partners with us so that we can overcome loneliness and rejection.

Then through our holiness and His healing us, we can live for the glory that comes to God. The ripple effect of God's glory imparts glory to us, as well as to others.

Defenses are barriers to intimacy because our own pain or suffering stands sentinel to guard the door of our heart. God has given us His heart, His loving Son Who has led the way into love and past suffering and through our defenses and again to sense and know His presence. Our Father delights in us! We are the joy of His heart! It is both a privilege, and an honor to Him as well as to us, to tackle the thorny issue of our defenses.

Taking on our defenses is like picking berries in a briar patch. It will pay off, but we're going to pay for it! *To heal defenses, we have to become willing to suffer for the sake of love. Our love for God motivates us, and we draw strength from His love for us.* Through Him, we embrace love for ourselves. With His help we can remove these barriers to intimacy with Him and within ourselves.

When the self defends against the self, the use of such internal defenses is a reenactment of the original rejection from the outside. When pain, fear, threat, helplessness, hurt, rejection, anger, tender feelings, or wanting to cry are not welcome within the self, a defense is exerted. We pressure ourselves to disallow, deny or minimize those feelings. *When we apply force against ourselves to abandon such inner feelings or thoughts we create self-abandonment, a self-rejection.* There can, however, be a necessary kind of defensive response within the self that is the equivalent of self-control and helpful self-discipline. People who want to sleep too much, eat too much candy, or express hostility without caring how it affects others, need help. They must seek to understand their underlying needs. Then they need to structure coping strategies to meet those needs. At the same time they have to stop acting out impulsive, avoidant, and withdrawing or aggressive defenses. This person needs help in accessing the underlying emotional fear, pain or anger that is being blocked by defensiveness.

What is necessary when dealing with defenses? The function of defenses within the self is to avoid pain. Aggressive defenses are no exception. When a person beats up on himself, it is for a reason. It is to avoid a deeper hurt. The solution to defensiveness is counter intuitive. We must be willing to experience our hurt. Pain-avoidance was the very reason for the formation of the defense in the first place.

The Will To Heal – A Healing Of Defensiveness

We cannot heal emotionally without plunging again into the very event, relationship, and feelings that hurt us in the first place. Reexperiencing occurs very often in the reprocessing of the buried trauma, the feeling is that the event in the past is happening with more clarity and emotional reality than we experience in our awareness of our present surroundings. The fear, the vulnerability, the helplessness, the lack of control over what injured us, sometimes sheer panic or terror or the sensations of violence or abuse stored as body memories; these need to be welcomed into consciousness when we are secure enough and have a safe environment to experience them again. The will to heal involves the will to experience pain which we have stored in ourselves unprocessed. EMDR (Eye Movement Desensitization and Reprocessing) is a therapy that has been developed since the mid-1980's by Dr. Francine Shapiro which powerfully affects the ability to reprocess trauma which has been dissociated and stored in memory. EMDR provides one of the powerful therapeutic tools in overcoming defensiveness and healing emotions damaged through trauma.

Healing intent requires a new set of instructions to the self:

1. Feel your pain. Find out what hurts you. Get whatever help you need to do this.

2. Understand the beliefs you've lived by that have enabled you to survive. Defensive beliefs attached to your pain are faulty. Identify what they are. These are what you want to stop.

3. Determine opposite beliefs and ideas to replace faulty beliefs. These are what you want to start.

4. Take a new approach to fear, panic and the fear of terror. Investigate it don't avoid it!

5. Welcome experiences that trigger defensive reactions and troublesome emotions. Don't fight or resist them. Watch what you say to yourself so that you welcome what's difficult. You can't heal what you don't see!

Use such signals for pain and fear as a door you can go through, a door to the place where feelings and memories are stored. Going through that door can provide you with the memories of experience so you can have access to the things that have hurt you. Then you can grieve. When grieving has fully finished its course, the painful feelings attached to the original memory will be gone. When the hurt is grieved about and the loss is accepted, then you will be free. The fear of fear and the fear of pain will be gone. The defense leaves when the grief is finished regarding any specific event. When a person is able to feel grief and accept losses, the need for defenses against the self disappears.

SELF UNDERSTANDING THROUGH VENTILATING STRESS

When we are willing to experience our hurt, then we can journey to the place of our pain. Once we've repressed our pain, the connections to our original experience are often blocked. It's like being locked out of our own home. So a search must be made to find out what's bothering us. If you know yourself reasonably well, you might have a list of potential trouble spots about which you can ask yourself, "Is this what's bothering me?" A person who gets migraine headaches due to emotional stress might ask: "Does it have to do with work – money – anger – husband-wife relationship – children – mother-father relationship – friend – rejection?" If we asked ourselves those questions and paused, reflecting at each of the potential trouble areas, we would get some emotional confirmation about whether or not this is the trouble spot by the tension we feel or the intensified emotional reaction we feel while thinking about that particular area. Once we find the general area, we need to find the specific area that bothers us.

Another way to find out what's bothering us is to act in expressive ways that discharge the physical tension or stress that our bodies are carrying in ways that connect us with the underlying emotion. One such way is called a bio-energetic exercise. If your body is in good condition, and there are no medical reasons why you shouldn't do this exercise, lie down on a mattress so that you're facing up. Then you lift your legs one at a time, knees straight, and forcefully bring them down on the mattress. Making fists, you slam your arms down, so that your full arm hits the mattress. Your arms and legs should be operating in a rhythmical fashion so that an opposite arm and leg are slamming the mattress at the same time. While slamming, let yourself yell or say short bursts that express feelings. Say whatever comes to your mind. Such as, "It's not fair!," "You have no right!,"

"I'm angry, I'm furious!"

Continue to express and ventilate the anger until you don't feel angry any more. Once your anger is spent, allow yourself to let the pain come up while continuing the exercise. What happens is that often, people start crying and connect with what has hurt them. Continue the crying and expression of the hurt until the pain is discharged. Grieving is essential for healing.

SELF-ACCEPTANCE AND DEFENSES

Being defensive is the opposite of being self-accepting. The changes from personal defensiveness to self-acceptance require a re-creation of the self structure. Where an abandonment of the self has occurred because we have chosen to defend against our feelings about our experience, we must now intend to open ourselves to our feelings about our experience. We begin a process of self-nurture, of healing, and assert a positive presence of our selves to our injured self. We say to our hurt self, "It's OK, I'm here to be with you, to understand you, to hear how you feel. I'm interested in you. I won't get frightened by your pain. I won't run away. I won't get angry with you. If you've done something wrong, we'll figure out how to fix it or do what's right. I'm here and I won't leave you. I love you."

This stance toward the self is the opposite of one we took earlier when the defense was formed. It is the opposite of the way we perceived our world responding to us, which we internalized in a defensive positioning of ourselves against ourselves. The new stance is one of self-nurture, of being present with yourself. This attitude toward the self is the one which mirrors the presence of the Holy Spirit, the "paraclete," the Comforter. "Paraclete," the word for the Holy Spirit in the Greek New Testament, literally means "One who comes alongside." The Holy Spirit presences Himself with us in our pain for the purposes of healing us, letting us know we are not alone and providing grace and mercy.

I've heard people say, "I'm defensive, so what?" People who think this way think of defenses as something that affects only their relationships with others, but doesn't affect them. Their attitude seems to be, if it affects only their relationship with others, they can live with it.

The "so what" to defensiveness is that damage cannot occur in relationships with others without deeply affecting the self. One example is when people are embarrassed to cry in front of somebody else, and stop themselves from crying when they are feeling hurt. I have often asked them, "Do you cry when you are by yourself and you are hurt?" Usually, if people will not cry in my presence, they will not cry by themselves, either. I have found that when people work through their defenses against shame or weakness and learn to be comfortable crying in my presence, they are then more comfortable crying and processing the grief they feel about their emotional pain when by themselves.

Defenses create distance. Barriers to intimacy are formed between the self and others, the self and God, and the self and the self. Defenses that are the barriers to intimacy need to be dismantled, for intimacy occurs in a love relationship only when we take down the barriers that separate us.

Self-Boundaries And Defenses

Defenses are different from boundaries. Defenses may reflect boundaries of the self. Boundaries are a necessary part of self definition, of ownership of the self, and the space of the self and the differentiation between the self and others. They are a necessary part of the respect for ourselves and others. Boundaries define what I am and what I am not, what I feel and do not feel, what I have and do not have, what is mine and not mine. They define what you are and what you are not. They define the limits of my space and your space, my being and your being. Boundaries are an essential basis for respect, both for ourselves and for others.

Eleanor had a paper route when she was a young girl. Her father took all the money she earned and used it for family expenses. It vaguely bothered her that she had little that belonged only to her. After all, it was all she knew. Who is she? What belongs to her? Is she a separate person, or does she just belong to others? What does she expect from herself and others? What do they have a right to expect of her? Does she have a right to say no, or is she required to do whatever someone else wants of her as long as she has the ability or energy?

I have great empathy for Eleanor, because I was raised with a very different kind of respect for me. I too had a paper route when growing up. The money I earned was always mine to keep, either to save or to spend. When

I was in fifth grade, I earned enough money to buy a camera and photographic equipment. We each learn differently, based on our own life experiences. Because she didn't have respect for her limits of money and time, unclear self boundaries became a needed issue for her over rights to her own money, time, and with male authority. Because I was respected in these areas, I didn't have those boundary issues. I've shared already about the boundary issues I did develop regarding ideals and approval expectations.

Our defenses exist at the place where we have self-boundaries between ourselves and others. If we have no clear definition of our boundaries, we have no clear right to protect ourselves. If we do not protect ourselves appropriately and make the best decisions about us because our boundaries are unclear or we feel we do not have rights to boundaries, we can allow ourselves to get hurt. Then we need to listen to the inner signals we get when we feel hurt or angry. Those signals send us a message that we need to develop different boundaries in order to defend ourselves appropriately. It bothers Eleanor that life seems to be such a fight and that she feels anger so much of the time. Even though distressing, it is necessary to go through such a process until she has a greater sense of ownership of what belongs to her, greater clarity about her limits and boundaries and she doesn't automatically allow herself to be intruded on and hurt so much.

WHOLENESS, A RESTORATION OF INTIMACY

Defenses indicate our separation, a brokenness, a splitting within the self. There are necessary defenses both within the self and between ourselves and others as long as we and others are not whole. In every way in which we have defenses active in our relationships with others or ourselves, we also defend against intimacy with God. Intimacy occurs when we let our defensive barriers come down. Only then can we fully know God, ourselves, or others. As human beings we long to be known for who we truly are, accurately, deeply, fully and lovingly. God has provided us pathways to healing, a working through our defenses that prevent our connection with the most painful and difficult parts of ourselves. He invites us into that task with great delight, because He knows we cannot be fully successful even at accomplishing our own healing without our coming to know Him. We cannot fail to benefit from this journey away from defensiveness toward wholeness and intimacy, because the person "who loves God is known by God."[3]

---

1   Isaiah 53:4

2   Romans 5:8

3   1 Corinthians 8:3

Chapter 4

Hidden Personal Needs

༝

*"Happy are those who find refuge in you, whose hearts are
set on pilgrim roads. As they pass through the Baca valley,
they find spring water to drink. Also from pools the Lord
provides water for those who lose their way...
For a sun and shield is the Lord God, bestowing all grace
and glory. The Lord withholds no good thing from those
who walk without reproach. O Lord of hosts, happy are
those who trust in you!" Psalm 84:6-7, 12-13 (NAB)*

EMOTIONALLY LOST

Humility accepts our hidden personal needs. Being needy and *not* knowing it is like being lost. We often don't know the way to replenish the parts of ourselves that are thirsty, hungry, tired or hurting.

Personal needs make us feel vulnerable, as though needs equals weakness. We'd rather hide them. Needs can be conflicted, demanding, or inconvenient. They reveal a lack. They force us into dependency on God, others, ourselves, or into a position against our needs. People sometimes interpret their needs as evidence of inadequacy, that something's wrong with them. A simple need sometimes makes some people feel unsafe and leads them to hide under beds or in mental closets. Jenna puts her needs this way. "I don't have a voice. It's as though I'm shouting for help and no one's coming. It's a desparate feeling!" One of the most intense needs we have is our need to feel loved.

Previously, I've talked about defenses. When I see people acting out their defenses by carrying bitterness or unforgiveness, by engaging in pornography or acting our sexually, I ask people to search for the hidden personal need. We need to end the defensive distortion and we need to provide for the legitimate need.

Because He cherishes us, God is willing to provide for us while we accept our needs. "You open your hand and satisfy the desires of every living thing."[1] Our receiving from Him is a step toward our being able to cherish and value ourselves – a step toward self-esteem.

Barb is a Christian friend. She shampooed her client's hair when she experienced something remarkable. God's joy bubbled up within her and she knew that it was God's feeling toward her client. Sadly, her client had difficulty believing that God could be smiling on her. Out of the resources which we have first received ourselves, we will be able to nourish other thirsty souls with life-giving water which comes from the eternal springs of God's generous Spirit. Happiness and fulfillment result from such inner healing.

STRESS SURFACED THINGS HIDDEN FROM ME

I had just had a rough day. When I got home I told my wife, Chris, I'd like to do some prayer to help in my own healing process. I needed it! I asked her whether she'd pray with me about it. Prayer can be used just as therapy can, to process emotions and experience emotional and spiritual healing.

That day, a patient let me know in no uncertain terms how little he thought he was getting from me in therapy. This felt rejecting because I had extended myself to him with as much energy as I could. Now please understand, he was just doing his job as a patient. The patient's job in a therapy relationship is to recreate the conflict which he or she hasn't yet solved. If the person has puzzle pieces missing, maybe the therapist has them. Or maybe a new picture of wholeness can emerge through the therapy relationship. Or perhaps, the person will find out what he dreads to find out, which is that the problem can't be solved at all. If the therapist can't deal with it, the patient is tempted to believe that the problem is not fixable.

This person gave me his problem. That's how I interpreted what happened. I felt blasted. That is, he made me feel it. Now I had to struggle with the same feelings that he had. What he gave me was personal rejection and hopelessness about his situation ever changing. A therapist can often hear these feelings without taking personal responsibility for them or for causing them. If a therapist is able to hear the feelings without taking them in, that's the healthful thing to do. If there are unresolved areas the therapist has, then some of the other person's projected feelings will get in, without the therapist's necessarily knowing about it. That's what happened to me. I personalized and accepted the other person's feelings as belonging to me. I felt sadness, emotional pain, and I felt "off-centered" and didn't know why. I'm sure you know that other people besides therapists fall for this – taking feelings from others that don't belong to them.

When Chris and I prayed, I told God I felt deeply injured after the session. I asked Him, "What are You trying to heal in me?" I started feeling a deep sadness and let myself cry. As I cried, I had the feeling: "I can't stand this!" I also had the impression that I didn't know what to do about this but take it. As I said that, it evoked the memories of my sister and me arguing as children and the impression I got as the oldest child, that I was supposed to be able to control the "fighting." The feeling that "I didn't know what to do but take it" seemed reminiscent of those encounters with my sister at a younger age. I thought I was to take something that I considered abusive without replying. That was what I thought as a child my parents had wanted from me. It was that feeling which I couldn't stand. I was still reacting emotionally as though I needed to allow things to happen to me and protect my parents by my silence. "Just taking it in silence" doesn't allow me to value myself properly, as equal in value to others. Sadness and pain cannot help but be the product of such situations.

Such attitudes seldom get brought into the light of consciousness without going through a painful trigger event. If we react to such situations only defensively, then we cannot grow and be healed by learning the truth about ourselves and experiencing our emotions. Suffering has the ability to change what I value and esteem by testing it, bringing unresolved problems into clear focus. What's the alternative? I can harden myself by angry, self-justifying reactions, and drive my pain deeper into hiding.

To Heal My Hidden Pain, I Focused On God As My Strength

Inner hurt cannot be ignored if we are to heal. We must fully experience our pain and discharge it through grief. Expressing it helps immeasurably!

It is a helpful part of healing to bring those mourning feelings into God's presence and come into the shelter of His protection. As we bring to God our painful feelings, and even our complaints, we refocus on Him. This day, as I finished fully pouring my heart out to God, my focus could shift more fully to the One to Whom I was talking.

The Holy Spirit kept bringing songs to our minds which we would sing. Then the Lord gave my wife a picture when I asked what He was trying to heal in me. Jesus was leaning down, scrubbing some brick steps. I understood the steps as Jesus doing some cleaning in me to advance me – going up the steps of humility. It was clear that He was serving me. To accomplish this, He was stooping over to do the scrubbing. I understood my present suffering as a necessary path in learning humility, as well as in esteeming myself properly. The brick was a personalized symbol for me, because we have brick steps leading into our house.

We believed that God was leading us to read through many psalms beginning at psalm one, to refocus on God and nourish our bruised souls and injured spirits. We ended at psalm eighteen. David the psalmist prayed and sang this song when God delivered him from his enemies and from King Saul who pursued and tried to kill him. "I love You, O Lord, my strength. The Lord is my rock, my fortress and my deliverer; my God is my rock, in Whom I take refuge. He is my shield and the horn of my salvation, my stronghold. I call to the Lord, Who is worthy of praise, and I am saved from my enemies." Then we got down to verse 35. "You give me Your shield of victory, and Your right hand sustains me; *You stoop down to make me great.*"[2]

This passage leapt out at me! I felt stunned, feeling full of gratitude as the enormity of what we just read hit me. There it was again! Jesus stooped down to make me great. Here is the God of the universe humbling Himself to serve me. I cried as this truth about Jesus' loving service to me penetrated my innermost being. I fully realize this isn't just for me. It's as individually personal to each of us as our names are different. It's His purpose for all of His children that they be blessed with greatness, that they be lifted up to their heavenly position as sons and daughters of God.

Greatness in God's kingdom is measured in loving service through humility. The only way for God to accomplish that was for Jesus to stoop down to me and serve me. This was Jesus, stooping down to clean my brick steps. I know that His gift of love is a very personal preparation for me, so I could learn to walk in humility. The trigger event was my patient's anger at me in the presence of my feeling that I had extended myself to him. A cleansing of my way, a scrubbing had to occur in me to make it possible for me to have a humble response. Jesus humbly served me so I could follow in His steps. His loving service cost Him more dearly than I can imagine. But He did not consider it suffering. He considered it a joy. As I began to take these truths in, my own pain began to be transformed into the joy of serving someone else in love. The scrubbing Jesus provided for me was through my upset patient. It wasn't pleasant, it was difficult. But it was healing, and it led me into a depth of knowledge of myself and of my relationship with God which I wouldn't otherwise have experienced.

EQUAL-OPPORTUNITY SCRUBBING

Jesus' scrubbing the steps was happening to my wife Chris that night as well. She too had been feeling stressed, "off-centered," and sad at the end of her work day. So she wanted to bring her own needs to God in prayer as well. A friend and assistant had decided to talk directly with their mutual boss about the vacation schedule. None of them was supposed to take vacation during peak times of busyness, which for most of them meant the summer. It was summer and things were action-packed at the office and they were short-staffed in the secretarial area because one person was on vacation. This secretary was feeling burnt out and crunched with an over-full work load. She had already taken her vacation months earlier. Chris had waited several months until the end of June to see whether she would have a window of time to squeeze in one week of vacation in early August, while there was a lull in her schedule. It seemed that this co-worker's complaint might threaten her vacation week. Chris wondered, "Why didn't she come to me before going to the boss? It would have saved a lot of misery for everybody." All five people affected in the department were called in to the boss's office.

As Chris prayed, she became aware of betrayal feelings and brought them tearfully before the Lord, willing to forgive what she felt was betrayal to her. But a part of her pain was fear. She was afraid that God would allow her August vacation to be taken away. Her fear was that if something was good for her she might lose it. This, no doubt, came from her times as a child with rheumatic fever and her prolonged confinement in bed, as well as one traumatic stay in the hospital at age five. This work situation brought up those old fears that maybe God didn't think her good enough to deserve good things. Could she count on God's wanting only good for her?

Her present pain gave access to an old hurt that still needed more healing. *She needed to know at an emotional level, not in her mind only, that she was loved and valued by God.* Her pain opened the door for her to receive more healing in an important area of her woundedness. Jesus came to her in a picture as she prayed. First, He said, "I, too, was betrayed by my friend." Then He said, "I have loved you with an everlasting love." In her prayer picture, Chris gave Jesus a big hug. He wrapped His arms around her in a strong embrace and held her. She let His love penetrate and soaked it in. In flowed the love and comfort she needed, as well as the confidence that her way and her future would be protected by a God who had only good in mind for her.

The pain of new injuries breaks open the pain of old wounds. The opportunity is created for the healing of both. *Such suffering is necessary in healing.* If we fight such pain in a defensive way, we do not allow the openness necessary for God's healing purposes to be accomplished. We need to trust in the strength that comes from God and the fact that He always intends good for us, no matter what our pain or suffering is. Adversity then does not drive us away from God, but makes us more open to God so that we too can say, "I love you, O Lord, my strength." We are no longer strong in ourselves, but God is our strength. David, when he was attacked by enemies, discovered that his own strength wasn't sufficient, but God's was.

When we know that we are loved, that God is good and always with us, we can shift our focus away from our injury to God. He constantly pours new energy, vitality and life into us. He sustains and strengths our well-being by His never ending stream of mercy.

MID-LIFE CRISIS

I am not trying to glorify suffering, as though it were intrinsically good. The process is painful, sometimes destructive, but the results can be beneficial. Here's the rest of my story that I said I'd share with you. At age forty I went through a mid-life evaluation. It was a life review. I looked at how I wanted my life to turn out, what I was doing that would help me get there, what I was doing that would prevent me from getting there and what needed to be lopped out of my life. I believed that I had accomplished my essential goals to that point and I looked at what else was most important to me. My mother's suffering was what I wished most I could do something about. Mother had begun using a wheel chair since I had graduated from college. At age nineteen, I had prayed for her healing. Back then, I thought that I had prayed fully in faith, and that God was obligated to heal her. Didn't the Bible say that if you asked in faith believing that you would receive, you would have what you asked for? But God didn't heal her. I felt betrayed by God. So I stopped asking Him for things. For twenty years I approached Him only with prayers of thanks. Not only was I aware of being concerned about my mother, but about the lack of fulfillment in my relationship with God and my withered, anemic prayer life.

I revisited this decision not to engage in proactive prayer. I talked with God again. I told Him that I felt betrayed that He hadn't healed my mother and that I still wanted Him to heal her. As I entered into this conversation with God, I thought my concern for my mother was completely selfless. All of my conscious thoughts and feelings had my mother as the object of my concern. Many weeks went by in which I re-explored through prayer issues about my mother's healing and reopened what was to become a dialogue with God. Through that intense prayer involvement, my psychological defenses started breaking open. What started as a mid-life evaluation escalated into a crisis. Mid-life crisis more accurately describes the scope and extent of my turmoil. I entered into some intensive inner work and used therapy extensively to help me.

A year and a half of painful emotional and spiritual struggle ensued. A friend commented when he saw me at church that he saw pain in my face. He thought I must be carrying too much of my patients' pain with me. But it wasn't theirs' he saw, but mine.

HIDDEN MOTIVATION

What emerged was the role of my personal needs in wanting my mother healed. I know that much of my feeling came from a profound empathy for her affliction and genuine wish for her well-being. But she was *my* mother. My *self* and my *needs* did play a part in my concern for my mother. The role my self played, at first, was completely hidden from me. That is, some of my self had been lost to me. At age forty, I was beginning to see my childhood needs for care that were missed because of my mother's illness. When a mother with five children gets M.S., a lot of the housework gets delegated to the children. It also seemed that her illness made her less emotionally available to us, and less able to handle conflicts, especially between my sister and me.

I began to see a hidden motivation in my readiness for my mother's healing. I was now ready to begin my own healing in issues that dealt with my own needs for affirmation, love, and nurture. I discovered that I was still attached to my mother in my achievement. My accomplishments were not just something that stood on their own. Rather, they were duties I performed to become worthy of my mother's love. If I were successful enough and had achieved well enough, I would be deserving of my mother's love. By my standards, I had been *that* successful. Now the unconscious part of my motivation became apparent. *It was now time for me to get what I needed for myself – love and worth!*

I had perceived achievement as the way to get my mother's love. I was ready for healing because I had done what I needed to do to achieve. In my unconscious mind, I thought I had now earned and now deserved her love, and I was ready to collect. But she wasn't in any condition to give. She still had her incapacitating illness. The thought that I could actually remake the situation so I would receive unconditional love in my present-day relationship with my mother is, of course, irrational. It's just that my mother was the first source of that love bonding so it's the place to which my unconscious naturally looked to fix the problem of my lack. The adult parts of myself had been functioning fine, but those energies were now needing to be redirected to loving and healing the hurting and needy child within.

God takes on Himself the responsibility of bringing me into the place of healing if I commit myself to Him and am willing to be healed. Even the best of human relationships are flawed and in need of repair and restoration. God used my mother's continuing illness to telegraph a message to me about my need for healing.

The dilemma is this: what if God had answered my prayer for my mother's healing? What would have happened to my own healing? Had she been physically healed, it would have tended to move me to a neurotic solution for my needs to be met without my realizing it. My motives for asking for her healing were defensive and self-centered in a way I had not yet recognized. I hadn't understood that God would be willing to heal simply because He loves us and had provided for it in the cross. God is in the position of being able to know what's best for all people concerned when there are competing or conflicting needs.

My mother's continued physical suffering had a redemptive and intercessory role on my behalf. One of the meanings of her suffering was that her illness not only created some of my lack, but helped contribute to my healing. People are limited and often cannot know how they affect others in important ways. They can only trust in God's goodness.

I, like others who wish personal healing, must go on a journey in life which reveals and discloses to us needs of which we were unaware. God the Holy Spirit as comforter and nurturer is involved in this disclosure process in order to bring wholeness. Once we know that we are thirsty, we can come to His eternal springs to drink. We will learn not to choke off parts of ourselves from that life-giving source – not to quench the Holy Spirit. As we have freely received, so we can freely give.

HEALING THE "ABORTED SELF"

I will share two people's experiences in growing from the false self to the true by learning about personal hidden needs and acting to take care of them. God often infuses us with hope through our dreams. Dreaming is one of the wonderful ways in which things hidden from our conscious minds percolate to the surface of our awareness. Once things are conscious, we can choose solutions to problems. In this, we can grow closer to God as well as to our real selves. Remember Eleanor? She reported in a dream, "I chose to have an abortion. It was a tiny and fully formed fetus, much tinier than a real fetus would be to be fully-formed. I even viewed the fetus after the abortion. The dream was connected with work in ministry I was being considered for. Because I had the abortion, I was no longer being considered for that ministry position. The most clear feelings resulting from the dream were guilt, regret and remorse."

I asked her what she thought it meant in her dream that she chose to have an abortion. She thought she was aborting herself. I noted the connection to ministry in her dream. I wondered, did her decision to abort herself mean that she no longer was being considered for a ministry position? I asked, "Has anything happened recently that would be the reason why you're having the dream now?" "Yes," she said. "I withdrew my name from being considered for a ministry position." She named the church. The dream is a powerful picture of how she feels about what she came to call, "aborting my ministry, my professional self." Why would she choose such a painfully wrenching experience? What led up to it?

In recent years, Eleanor had coped with people's having expectations of her by withdrawal and procrastination. She didn't allow herself to get into a situation where she would have to report to a pastor or be accountable. She was aware that this has also cost her the ability to gain emotional and spiritual support from peers. She feared excessive demands on her and lacked confidence in her ability to say no, or place appropriate boundaries on what she would agree to be responsible for. She described how she experienced ordinary expectations of herself. "I've been aware of times today that I was caught up in anxiety as though everything I have to do in the next couple of days had to be done right now. The feeling was one of overwhelmed, exhausted failure. The feelings were way out of proportion to what I have to do, so I am sure they are connected to something in the past."

What happened to her in the past that led up to these present feelings? She was a girl, and her father wanted a boy, and treated her like a boy. So she seldom experienced love and acceptance for who she was, and certainly not from her father because she was a girl. The part of ministry she entered was a "male world," since she was not in children's ministries, but rather is gifted to work with adults. So in a church ministry responsibility, she couldn't help but confront the painful reminders of what happened in a church internship where she experienced her role as a woman in ministry as not supported by her supervising pastor. Unfinished business about her feelings about being a woman in a man's world brought back issues about her lacking acceptance as a girl growing up.

As a child, she says, "I often felt exhausted." Her parents owned a gasoline station and store in which the family lived on the premises. A door to the store opened right into the dining room. Seven days a week the store was open and the kids were expected to work. "Seven in the morning until ten at night was too long a day for a kid," she emphasized. Boundaries for the self were not learned in her living environment or in her parents' work expectations. She doesn't remember even being allowed to go over to a friend's house to play. But if a friend's father needed help in getting the hay in from the field, she was allowed to help. She was never given parental permission to have needs or wishes, or to have fun. She's still needing to know that there's a difference between herself and the expectations of others. What she has learned still has a momentum in her life. She says, "I tend, even now, to keep on the move from early morning to ten or eleven at night."

Limitless expectations on herself caused a collapse during two earlier times of schooling, the first in nurse's training, the second in seminary. During seminary, for example, she attended full-time, taught two weekly classes, raised two teen-age daughters, had a "big house that my husband expected me to keep completely clean and in order," and was active in a couple of community organizations. After two semesters and an internship, she got exhausted, depressed, and had difficulty making decisions, at times becoming angry and volatile.

Love Restores The Aborted Self To Life

I think from a brief summary of her history you can see why she would make the painful choice to abort her professional ministry role in favor of God's healing her wounds first. She understands her therapy process as bringing to life and "raising up that aborted self." She works actively, energetically, and prayerfully on her own healing, including using therapy to that end. She is a woman of faith who knows that God intends her healing. She says, "Lord, I pray that You reveal to me what I need to ask You to heal in me." Her prayers for healing are in the process of being answered. Growing into the true self involves a community. Friends have begun to offer prayer support for her ministry. One therapist friend told her he keeps a prayer journal and offered for her to call his voice mail and leave prayer requests as often as she needs to. "So many people are willing to place value on what I'm saying. I've had so little practice at this," she says, somewhat surprised.

She noticed a change in her husband. She said, "I really sensed love. He is really valuing who I am and has let go of his need to coerce me." She illustrated the previously conditional nature of his love from a conversation with him. "When I'm not exercising the way you want me to, you don't love me in that moment." Her husband's changing how he expressed his love encouraged her. She, too, was changing what she was asking him for, "I need to have that kind of unconditional love from you. That's not an inappropriate need."

She shared her struggles about how she has felt as a woman in a male-dominated field with a male friend in ministry. He gave her a big hug and said, "I love you just for who God created you to be." She related this experience with tears in her eyes, saying how much that unconditional support and love meant to her and acknowledging the pain of how little she has felt that in her life.

DESPERATE FOR LOVE

Friends persuaded Henri Nouwen to expose the raw places in his soul for others to see by publishing his secret journal. He says that life came crashing down on him over a seven month period of extreme anguish. He lost "his self-esteem, his sense of being loved, his hope for healing, and his trust in God." What triggered this? He said that a deeply satisfying friendship became his "road to anguish." When people were assuring him of their love and appreciation, he experienced himself "as a useless, unloved and despicable person."

He writes speaking to himself. "What is your pain? It is the experience of not receiving what you most need. It is a place of emptiness where you feel sharply the absence of the love you most desire. To go back to that place is hard because you are confronted there with your wounds as well as with your powerlessness to heal yourself.

"Whenever you feel lonely, you must find the source of this feeling. You are inclined to either run away from your loneliness or dwell in it....You might find that your loneliness is linked to your call to live completely for God....You may find your loneliness not only tolerable but even fruitful.

What seemed primarily painful, may be a feeling that, though painful, opens to you the way to an even deeper knowledge of God's love."[3]

Victoria shows us another path in becoming the true self. She too needed humility when she discovered needs she had tucked away, and found unwanted and unknown feelings. Feelings can be God's alarm clock arousing us from unconscious slumber. "Nothing but numbness," that's how Victoria described the mask over her sadness on what should have been one of the happiest days of her life. "I was wearing a beautiful dress on my wedding day," she said. "Life has not been satisfying. Life has been hurry-up for forty-two years. I'd almost like to keep going in that mode rather than acknowledge the deficit. I don't want to go through the grief and mourning – facing squarely the truth that my life has been lacking in joy." She supposed that it was her fault. I asked her, "Why might you want to keep this up?" She pictured herself in the patio of her parent's back yard, "feeling comfort, lying down with the cold rocks against my face. I'm afraid to experience warm comfort," she explained. She has taken comfort in the coldness of not feeling.

Then she pictured the athletic trophies she had won, and saw herself holding a big silver platter with engravings of her triumph. She shook her head, holding the trophy in her mind's eye, feeling cold. "I feel like all my family members surround me and say, 'Good.' I relax in the cold comfort," she said. "I feel sad."

At a Christian charismatic conference, two people who prayed for her said they had received a word from the Lord for her. The first person, a man, told her: "Forsake letting the words of man dictate how you live. Let them go and run from them, embracing the words of God, and letting the words of God be your foundation." His words were urgent. "Run from the words of man! If someone gave you a loaded gun that you knew would kill you, you'd drop it and run." I think he was telling her that she empowered other people to control her life. Sometimes their words were like a loaded gun, if aimed against herself. But she had withdrawn from people to keep them from influencing her. A second person, a woman, "had a vision of me behind a counter. I had put something between me and other people. I had missed blessings because I've been behind the counter, and the Lord is encouraging me to jump over the counter and dive in there." Her response to these prayer words was, "Oh Lord, I try so hard to stay close to you. Have I been so blind that I have missed blessings? I have been feeling like I am in the desert. Has it been my own blindness that I have missed blessings that I have really needed? I just feel sad."

Not long after, Victoria had gotten home and was feeling pleased with the clothes she had bought for her children that day. When she was going to put them away, she couldn't find the bag. She retraced her steps back to the telephone booth where she made a phone call and then checked with "lost and found" at the department store. Nothing. She waited in line at customer service at the store. By the time she got up to the head of the line and could speak with the person at the counter, she was crying so hard she couldn't talk. All she could manage to do was to push her driver's license across the counter and leave a phone number so they could talk with her later. She was glad she was wearing dark glasses so no one could see how hard she was crying. As she cried, she knew she needed to cry.

She knew that the intensity of her feelings was greater than losing some clothes would warrant. It was easier to give herself permission to feel sad about something her children might lose than to feel sad for herself. When she got home, she found the bag of clothes she had lost. She had put the clothes in the place where she would normally put them, but had just thought she hadn't put them there yet. It was then that she realized that she was unconsciously looking for a reason to cry. She had not been treating herself as though her own feelings of sadness and her needing to grieve were important. She was going through a breakup and loss of a relationship with Clyde, a man she had been dating, with whom she had developed a friendship. She was hurting inside. Not stifling her tears about the clothes connected her with the more important source of her pain, which was not far beneath the surface, her breakup with Clyde.

Victoria's crying was an awakening. She had let her feelings fall asleep through emotional numbness. Because she learned to keep silent about her own needs and feelings in her family, paying attention to what they would approve of, she did not welcome her hurt, painful or sad feelings. Not only were they unpleasant, they were inconvenient in what she wanted to achieve and inconsistent with the image she held of herself as a strong person who is in charge of herself. Weak emotions were not permitted! Numbness was better! Now she was learning that pain is the other side of joy. If she was going to experience the joys and satisfactions she would like from life, and that God intends to release, she needed to acknowledge and grieve about her pain. She determined to go through the life experiences necessary to heal the difficulties Jesus told her about earlier when He communicated them to her, as in an encouraging "love letter." They were impressions of what she believed Jesus was saying while she was writing in her personal journal.

> *Dear Victoria,*
> *Oh, how I love you. You are valiant and brave. You are the apple of my eye. Truly, you have had difficult mountains to cross. Truly, the way has seemed full of trials. Give your burdens to Me. When you feel like calling Clyde reach for this letter and meditate on My promises. You cannot fathom your own heart. I alone know it. Forgive yourself. Love yourself. There have been powerful forces at work — you must protect yourself by covering yourself in My blood daily. Give Clyde to Me. Let him go. No longer burden yourself with the relationship. You are free, cleansed, and forgiven. When you want to reach for a friend, reach for Me for I alone am able to fill you and heal you. Reach for Me. Little lamb, I love you. I give you peace.*

---

1   Psalm 145:16
2   Psalm 18:1-3, 35 (italics added)
3   Henri J. Nouwen, *The Inner Voice of Love.* New York: Doubleday, 1998; pp. 26, 36, 37.

I Pray That You Gain Life's Prize

꒰

This is my prayer for you. If you can pray it for yourself, please do.

*I pray that you grow rich and joyful
in the gentle and kind, forgiving love of Jesus.
Since you first need to receive what you give,
I pray for delightful times of soaking in His extravagant love.
So you will be washed, healed, purified, filled, and restored.*

*I pray that you will draw near to God's heart
and take personally His tender affection for you.
I pray that you will feel deeply His intimate love
that is beyond grasping with your mind.*

*I pray that the nail prints of Jesus
so mark your soul
with costly love beyond yourself
that you will give your best when it hurts.*

*I pray for a humility so pure
that God's love flows unobstructed.
I pray, above all you'll become known
as a person who loves.*

*May God-love drive you to grateful worship!
May people-love make you generous!
May self-love make you so glad to be you
that loneliness is impossible!*

*I ask God to enter your isolation in hardship,
your indignities in abuse,
your friendlessness in neglect, and
your mini-deaths in suffering.*

I ask that God's presence transform wounds
of emptiness, pain, fear, darkness, hiding, and shame.
May these become oases, springs in the desert,
filled with the overflow of God-refreshing, life-giving comfort.
How deep are your difficulties?
So deeply may Christ be formed in you!
Have defenses trapped you?
May love free your strength
from protecting what's been broken.

I assert before God…
that every adversary must bow the knee
before God's purposes in your life.

I pray that the new you will grow
until you are so like Christ in every way
that you are fully free to be yourself.

May you bathe in His lavish love,
enter covenant with His goodness,
seek intimacy in His friendship,
enjoy esteem from His respect,
renew hope in His faithfulness,
endure patiently for His purposes,
and inherit abundance
from His glory.

I say before God…
That you are His masterpiece!
You are His work of art that reflects His timing,
His watchfulness, and His ability to overcome evil with good.

I ask before God…
You'll be proof of His presence to those blindly searching,
unseeing through tears, bitten by cynicism or numbed by despair.

I affirm for your life…
You're created and gifted,
God called you by name, to bear His own nature.
In a world that's been lost,
He'll restore what's been damaged,
to bring Him great fame, and
give you great glory from His Ultimate worth.
For He is your prize, the reward of your journey.

Appendices

God Requests Your Personal RSVP

ꝫ

A Prayer Of Destiny

If you would like to commit to having all of your worth be established in God, I invite you on His behalf to pray this prayer. Then, I encourage you to go for your destiny. Become Christlike in all you are and do, through the empowering and enlivening work of His Spirit in you.

> *"Lord Jesus Christ, I stand before You forgiven because of Your gift. You have asked me to love as You do, with heaven's love. So transform my heart with all that's eternal. By myself, I'm not capable of such love. Please remind me through Your Holy Spirit to draw on Your resources when I am tempted to rely only on mine. Enable me to receive and bask in Your love. Please increase my faith so I will be empowered to love others beyond measure with your limitless love.*
> *"I ask You Father ...*

❀ *Enable me to love God with my whole being: heart, soul, mind and strength.*

❀ *Enable me to love others equal to Your love for me.*

❀ *Enable me to love beyond my power as a human being alone.*

❀ *Give me the passion to worship You above all else.*

❀ *Give me the thirst to constantly seek Your presence.*

❀ *Give me the delight in knowing the depth of Your heart.*

❀ *Enable me to lead others to know Your love.*

❧   *Help me to see myself through Your eyes. I know Father, that you love me equally as You love Your Son, Jesus. Father God, You view me as holy and pure because I am dressed in Jesus' pure and spotless garments. Thank You that I do not come before You with shame even when I am broken by sin. Your Word cleanses me every time I ask forgiveness and determine to change my ways to heaven's ways.*

"Lord Jesus Christ, I give You all that I am for You to create in me my destiny in You – eternal worth. You've gifted me to bless and benefit others, in Your Church, in the world and in the rest of Your creation. I give You all the life I have left for You to express Your life through me.

"I place You, Father, Son and Holy Spirit above all else in my life and above every other relationship. I place all of my worth on You – I worship You. You put me here on earth to bring You pleasure and glory. Thank You for delighting in me. Thank You for the overflowing joy I can find in Your presence!

"You are my Ultimate Worth. I trust You to establish the Ultimate Worth of Your goodness and glory in me forever. My worth can come from You alone! I also ask for Your Ultimate Worth to spill over into generations after me because You live in me, and I live in the world."

_____   _____
NAME   DATE

I'd be interested in knowing if you made this commitment. Russ Llewellyn.

Your Relationship With God

❧

Steps In Establishing And Maintaining A Personal Relationship With God

The Bible says some key things about establishing a relationship with God.

First, we all were created in His likeness as spiritual beings so we could have a relationship with Him.

Second, The self-centeredness of sin got passed down to us from our first human parents. Our own sin, as well as the sin we inherited, has separated us from the holy God who created us. This separation broke our relationship with Him.

Third, God sent His own Son, Jesus, to reestablish a relationship with us. Human sin causes death. Jesus died on the cross to pay that penalty. Because of sin, everybody dies. But Jesus rose from the dead so He can give everlasting life to those who believe in Him. That way, when people die, they go to heaven to live with God, rather than to stay separated from Him in life after earth.

Fourth, Jesus said that He is the *only way* we can enter a relationship with God. There is only one way, and not many possible ways to God the Father.

Fifth, we need to personally receive Jesus' death for us as God's loving gift to us.

Steps

1. Believe. Accept Jesus' death for you as God's personal gift to you.

2. Recognize what's wrong. Confess your sins to God through

prayer and tell God you're sorry for what you've thought, felt, said, and done.

3. ASK FOR, AND RECEIVE FORGIVENESS. Ask God to forgive you. Make it personal by receiving forgiveness for your sins through prayer. It does no good to confess your guilt if you don't receive forgiveness. Then, importantly, forgive yourself. If you don't forgive yourself, you're actually holding on to your guilt. You don't benefit from God's forgiveness until you forgive yourself.

4. CORRECT WHATEVER YOU CAN. When you've done wrong that has harmed others, talk to people, apologize, ask forgiveness, and make amends and restitution if it is possible or needed and won't bring further harm.

5. CHANGE LIFESTYLE DIRECTIONS. Make the decisions you need so you can live the way God wants you to. He gives you this guidance in the Bible, which is His word to you.

6. PUT JESUS IN CHARGE OF YOUR LIFE. Live by faith in Jesus and do what He says. Read, think about, and study His word, the Bible.

7. RECEIVE HIS HOLY SPIRIT. Ask God to come into your life to put the life of His Spirit within you. Then, ask Him to fill you with His presence and give you the power to live a holy life that pleases God. Begin to communicate with God through prayer, developing a relationship and an intimate friendship with Him. Ask Him for the things you or others need. Ask Him to correct what you see that's wrong.

Suggestion: You may simply pray to God the words below as a model for developing your relationship with God.

YOU MAY PRAY ...

I affirm, God, that You are good and have sustained me until this moment. (Col. 3:16.) Thank You, God, that You say to people, "I have loved you with an everlasting love; I have drawn you with loving-kindness.

(Jer. 31:3.) It is Your merciful love that keeps people from being consumed by how pure you are – the fire of Your holiness. Thank You that Your compassions are fresh every morning. (Lam. 3:22, 23).

I RECOGNIZE WHAT'S WRONG.

Thank You that You have made provision for everything that is wrong with my life, for all of my sin, and for everything in my life that falls short (Romans 3:23) of Your loving perfection and holiness.

I AGREE WITH YOU, GOD, about what has no life in me.

God, You've said that sin pays harsh wages, and that those wages are death. (Rom. 6:23). There are choices I've made, acts I've done, things that I've said, felt and thought that are wrong, hurtful, self-serving and unloving. There are things wrong with me personally and which I cannot change without Your help. These things are sin which keep me separated from You and from myself. They keep me from being able to please You or live in an open relationship with You.

I ASK YOUR FORGIVENESS, GOD.

God, You say that if we confess our sins, You are "faithful and just and will forgive us our sins and purify us from all unrighteousness." (1 John 1: 9). Please forgive me for all my sins.

I RECEIVE YOUR FORGIVENESS, GOD. I am willing to forgive myself.

Please help me to like and love myself when I don't like what I have done or what I have been. Help me not to hold grudges against myself or others. Help me not to beat myself up inside for past mistakes or failures.

I AGREE WITH WHAT YOU SAY, GOD, that my false and sinful self died with Christ on the cross. Because it is dead, I will be able to stop living sinfully. (Rom. 6:6). When I do things I don't want to do, or things that are wrong, help me to recognize, confess, and stop that path. Help me to walk in forgiveness, cleansing and Your new life by the power of Your Spirit, (Rom. 6:8).

I AGREE WITH YOU GOD that Your purpose for me is to live with You now and forever, because "the gift of God is eternal life through Jesus Christ our Lord." (Rom. 6:23).

I TRUST YOU, GOD that You will complete the work You started in me. (Phil. 1:6).

HERE'S GOD'S PROMISE TO YOU:

Romans 10:9, 10 says: "That if you confess with your mouth, 'Jesus is Lord,' and believe in your heart that God raised him from the dead, you will be saved. For it is with your heart that you believe and are justified, and it is with your mouth that you confess and are saved." Also, Romans 10: 13 says: "Everyone who calls on the name of the Lord will be saved."

SOME SUGGESTIONS AND IDEAS ABOUT YOUR PRAYER

Tell someone else (hopefully someone who will be supportive of you) that you have asked Jesus to forgive you and have put Him in charge of your life. You can be sure that God will keep all of His promises to you.

As You talk to God, it may be helpful to name or write down the specific sins You are asking Him to forgive. Once you've asked Him to forgive you, try not to keep revisiting these mistakes, and consider the truth that they are forgiven.

The confession and forgiveness step is needed to establish an initial personal relationship with God. We also need to use this step to cleanse us when we sin. When we confess sin, we need to forsake the sin and set up our lives and circumstances to help us be successful so we won't be tempted by the same sin. Also, we need to try to repair any damage that we've done, receive forgiveness, and walk in continual friendship and communication with God. When you ask forgiveness, receive it with gratitude and be thankful. Then, forgive yourself. Don't demand that you must first change, or act differently, before you forgive yourself.

Would you let me know if you have prayed this prayer for the first time? I'd like to know!

Resources
to turn self-esteem into...

Ultimate Worth

BOOK 2

Gaining Life's Prize
Transforming Adversity into Glory

Life breaks us. It's easy to misinterpret these woundings. Some think God let these things happen to us because we are not worthy. Sometimes we conclude that we are defective in our core, or are "bad people" from which we cannot recover or change.

Evil intends adversity to minimize and devastate your worth. But God uses adversity as a whetstone to sharpen His likeness in you and transform you into a person who reflects His Glory.

Our ultimate worth comes from what happens through us in the world. When the life of God and the glory of His love pass to you and through you to others, there is a ripple effect that can last throughout the generations. All that glory of God becomes part of your ultimate worth.

God can use all suffering, even the adversity of trauma, abuse and neglect for you to gain that prize that is in God alone—ultimate worth.

Ultimate worth is a prize worth gaining in life, even through suffering!

– Forward by Graham Cooke, Author and Speaker

Whole Person
PUBLICATIONS

Resources
to turn self-esteem into...

Ultimate Worth

BOOK 1

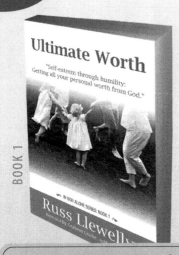

Ultimate Worth
"Self-esteem through humility:
Getting all your personal worth from God."

Russ Llewellyn
Forward by Graham Cooke...

> **Ultimate Worth**
> Self-esteem through humility:
> Getting all your personal worth from God

God allows but one path to permanent worth: love through humility. We build our self-esteem only on the things which God values. We recognize that apart from God, any esteem we give ourselves will crumble and scatter like dust swept away by the winds of time.

Our ultimate worth, our self-esteem, comes through humility. In humility, we learn to receive all of our personal worth from God. We learn to love and worship God, as well as love and respect ourselves and others the way God does.

God made you out of spirit, the same essence as He is. He made you for a noble purpose, to be and live on earth as sons and daughters of the Most High. You have a birthright, a kingly inheritance from God that lasts forever. Come to Him to receive the glory that comes in God alone – ultimate worth.

*Learn to see yourself
as God does!*

– Forward by Graham Cooke, Author and Speaker

Whole Person
PUBLICATIONS